'The Lords of the Mound did not leave this world because they were afraid of the sons of Abraham. They never left at all but rather, stepped aside to watch the doctrine of the mad manifest itself on the land. They did this as a lesson, so that the true folk of the Earth would eventually re-awaken to a deeper appreciation of the old ways.'

- Björn Hammarson

Dedication

For my Teacher

May there always be steel upon the stones, Wataan.
And may there always be a fire burning bright wherever you fare.
Corva Ellensdottir

A Voice from the Thornwood
The parting words of a Shar Master

by Shaara Corva

Edited by
Cassandra Wolf & Jack Wolf

By Jack Wolf
All materials herein are © Jack Wolf 2019

Also by Jack Wolf
The Way of the Odin Brotherhood
The Thornish Path

Contents

Forward

The book you now hold is a legacy in action. It is a tale written by one person and completed through the actions of others who are related to her through fire, oath and blood, through tribal ceremony, tribal heritage and deep primal bonds. It is the completion of one adventure and the beginning of another, the continuation of a unique tradition which has been in the world now for a good many years.

This story was given to us by our Hearth-kin and kinswoman Carolyn Ellensdottir, otherwise known by her Thornish name, Corva (the actual Thornish spelling of this name is Qorva; however Carolyn preferred the more Latin spelling as a nod to our corvine brothers.) It tells of her journey as a young woman and the deep spiritual awakening she experienced as she travelled across Canada in a quest to understand her purpose in life. Ultimately she found her purpose on the west coast, amongst a group of pagan people who followed an older way.

Corva's tale came to us as a stack of spiral-bound notebooks which were passed along after her death and which, unfortunately, spent years in storage along with other items from the past. Early in 2013, during a move, these notebooks were rediscovered.

We decided to fulfill the dream of our friend and tribal sister to one day have her chronicle published in book form. Corva took copious notes and although she tells us that she had not thought to write a book until later in her adventure, it would seem she took nothing for granted. Our efforts to assemble this work into a publishable form were made all the easier because of her attention to detail.

As we assembled all of the notes and various side-scribblings into book form it was necessary for us to add our own 'voices' to the chorus. As a result what you see here is really the combined effort of three Thornish people in action.

As Hearth-kin to Corva we have done our best to see her work finally come to light, though as editors and those who assembled the book we take only the smallest of credit. The magic and the inspiration that brought this work to life comes from our sister herself.

We hope that she is pleased, wherever she now fares in the world of spirit.

Jack Wolf & Cassandra Wolf
March 2015

Corva's Introduction

I have had many names in my life, some of them good, some noble and some not so much. It's the way of people like me, people who have chosen to walk the paths less traveled and to wend our way closer to the dark heart of Grandmother Earth.

The most powerful name I am known by is the one I consider to be my true name, my tribal name. It was given to me by my Wataan, my teacher.

When I was initiated I was given the name Corva. It honors the spirit of Raven and his mate, who have for a very long time guided me on my path. My full name is Corva Ellensdottir, which, according to the traditions of my tribal people, honors both my spirit and my mother.

In this tradition we are taught that the balance of nature and the laws of nature are of the greatest importance. We see ourselves as being tools of the Elder Kin. We see ourselves as implements of the laws of nature.

One of our sacred tools and symbols is a short-hafted spear called a Shar. As implements of balance we see ourselves as living Shar. Because of this, all initiated males are referred to formally as *Shar* and all initiated females as *Shaara*.

Another term we use to identify our culture is Thornish. We use this term with reference to our warrior ways and to the ordeal traditions that bind us together. I am Thornish. I am a woman of the Thornwood. I hold the Frith-knife.

Thus I am Shaara Corva Ellensdottir, Thornswoman of the Raven Lodge. I am the student of Agnes Maevesdottir (Master Ciarán) and Ari Torinsson (Master Raven) and a keeper of the sacred fire. I am also honored to be a blooded member of the Black Talon Society.

I should add that credit is certainly also due to those others who have aided me in my journey and these certainly include Oliver Moon, a respected local elder, his grandson Russell, and Russell's grandmother Annie Bear.

After a period of learning and training and of proving myself in this tradition I was elevated through ordeal and ceremony to the level of responsibility which we call the rank of Master. Masters are teachers and sages who carry the gift of our ways forward. And so, at the time that I write this, I am a Master in my tradition. I bear the blood-mark of my achievement.

I have decided to write this short book for three reasons. The first one is that my *Wataana*, my teachers, encouraged me to do this. I was very fortunate to have two teachers in this deeply pagan culture rather than just one, which is more traditional. My teachers told me that there are few of us in the world and that we should each endeavor to leave a record of our experiences. They told me that this is important because what we do, we do for the sacred Earth and that the Great Dark Mother is served not only through our acts in balance but also in teaching what we know. Before my elder teacher Raven's passing I told him I would write down some of what I know. This book represents that attempt.

The second reason I have for writing these things down is that I owe a debt of gratitude to my adoptive grandmother, Amber. Grandma Amber found me in a very dark place and set me on the road that would eventually lead me to my new family and tribe here in the west. Grandma encouraged me to pay it forward, as they say, to give to others in teachings and by example, rather than trying to pay anything back to those who taught us. As my Wataan taught me, we honor our teachers enough through our existence as strong Thornish people, as Shar.

The third reason is that I am dying.

There is an old bit of Thornish wisdom which tells us that when a warrior walks along she should always keep an eye out over her shoulder, that she should pause every now and then to see what is on the trail behind her. It is a wise thing, this little saying, because many things can sneak up on a person when they are not looking. And death is sneaking up slowly on all of us, no matter how wary we are.

A Master and Elder in our tradition, Raven's late friend Vala, once spoke of death as a disease which infects every single newborn baby and eventually kills every single human being who has ever lived. He said it was a disease that was 100% contagious to every human body and it was 100% lethal.

Master Vala was right about this. Some of us meet our end sooner rather than later. Some of us live long, healthy lives and are kind to our bodies throughout. Others through ignorance or spite do not do so well.

Some manage this path to death in a heroic way, like our dear Master Fox, or in a noble, almost legendary way like Black Coyote did…. or Master Raven, my noble elder teacher.

Others meet the gate-keepers to the spirit world in a more mundane way and I am sad to say that I am slated to be one of those people. I come originally from the east, from a city in southern Ontario. I worked for too many years in a factory where I was exposed to a great many poisonous things. I also developed the very bad habit of abusing tobacco as a young person and smoked cigarettes for many years. Suffice it to say that when I was younger I did a good many bad things to my body.

And so I am now told that there is a disease at work in my body which is gradually asking me to pay the toll for the things I did when I was young. The doctors want to inject me with more poison to see if it can be treated and if this doesn't work they want to expose me to doses of radiation.

To me this is like using water to help a drowning man.

I know that these so-called treatments are a sham. I know they will not work and instead they will reduce me to a shadow of myself. They will make me into a pathetic creature who will die on white sheets in a building full of strangers.

There is an elder who is a good friend to Raven and to many others in the valley where I came to live. He is very old and very knowledgeable in a lot of different ways but one of the things he is expert in is the ways of healing plants. He tells me that there are several of these sacred plant helpers that may heal me, but as the disease I have is quite far gone he is unsure if the plants will be able to help.

The elder, whose name is Tiva, has said that many people who die of this disease don't need to die, but the disease is brought on by the poisons of so-called modern civilization. He says he will do his best to help me and as he is a good friend to my teachers I trust him.

Wataan Raven called this wasting way of passing the *straw-death* and while no one in our tradition would ever think less of a member who happened to die in that way, it is not something that is preferred. How can there be any honor in such a thing?

I don't want to waste away. I would rather die doing something purposeful and of use.

Our songs do not tell of straw but rather of service and honor and being an implement of the First Law. They tell of firelight and kinship and of blood and of steel. They also tell of people who lived good lives and died in powerful ways.

They tell of legacies.

So I will not walk in that straw-death way. I will not let the white-coats experiment on me and watch me shrivel into a whispering, withered shell. Like my fellow Thornfolk who have passed beyond the gates before me I choose to keep control of my fate in that way.

I will walk what we call the Dokka, or more formally, the *Dokka 'Vor*, the long walk.

The Dokka takes many forms according to the one choosing it, and

I will not go into details about my own choices here. I explain myself in this way only so far as to say that there were three reasons for this book to be written and this is the third of them.

I believe that if we are to save our most sacred and beautiful world and the life-connections our world holds with so many other realities we need to further the education and awakening of as many worthies as we can. And to this act of reconnecting I will add my own voice.

Before Master Raven died he asked me to write down what I know and to teach what I know. By tradition we are asked to each take two students and pass along our knowledge to them in the best way we can. I have taught one student and have not taken a second. I might be able to consider this book a way to reach another…or several more. It is an important consideration when I write this.

I stayed in seclusion for too long after the passing of my elder Wataan. Master Ciarán advised me not to hide away and yet I didn't really listen to what she had to say. I know this now. It was a part of the old way that much of our tradition was hidden in seclusion, yet that way is changing. Now I must make up for my lack of presence in the place where our world meets the other side of the hedge.

In the past there used to be much secrecy about our way. The Elders were concerned with our knowledge being used by the wrong people or perhaps the name of our tradition being smeared in a bad way. Yet in later years this attitude changed, largely due to the efforts of a few people. Master Fox was one of these. He was the first of our Vardyr and for this alone he should be remembered with honor. Now the Elders and Masters are encouraged to speak more to the outside world of what it is we do. This is done with the hope of inspiring others to join us, or if not join us, become more awakened to the state of the world.

In this book I will tell my story, or what I can tell of it to those outside the thorn-hedge that separates those-who-know from those who do not, or who haven't fully awakened yet. I have my Master's permission to do that. I have the permission of our Elders to do that as well, and so I will.

I will do what I can before I am called to the darker trails, before I am called at last to my ancestors and indeed returned to the wise counsel and friendship of Master Raven.

I offer this book to those who are looking for a better way for the Earth. I offer it with enthusiasm to those who would like to do what they can to more fully wake up and to teach others about the healing of our world.

I am the product of my tribal traditions. I have added my stone now to the great Thornish hearth. What I have to say would never have been possible were it not for the many gifts that my tradition and the people of my tradition gave to me. As a result, though I might offer this book to those who might learn something from it I will also say that it is truly the property of my tradition, which is the way of the Thornish people, the Shar of the Black Talon Society. I expect that the contents of this work will be treated with respect.

They say that people live through the four seasons of life, beginning in the springtime with youth and young adults enjoying the fruits of summer. If this is true I imagine I am now in the deep autumn, going rapidly toward the winter of my life.

The gates of the Otherworlds beckon and day by day I can hear the voices of my Elders calling me home. I have much work to do before then, and so I will offer you, the reader, my wishes that you will find what you need in these pages.

Possibly we will meet again, in what we call *Us'ta'nor*, in the Fields.

May there always be steel upon the stones of your hearth

Shaara Corva Ellensdottir

Thornswoman of the Raven Lodge

October 1995

1. My Journey Begins

Ever since I was a little girl I have wanted to write. When I was small, so small I had barely learned to scribble letters on paper, I was frustrated because even then I knew that there was so much inside me that wanted to come out and be shared with the world. When people would ask me what I wanted to do when I grew up the answer would always be the same. I would say I wanted to be a writer. I wasn't even sure then exactly what kind of writer I wanted to be, or what kinds of things I would produce, but the thing I knew for certain was that I wanted to be a writer.

Sadly, like many people, I grew up in a world where people are programmed to kill the dreams of children and mold us all into creatures more fit for the plans of the great global machines. My parents, though I loved them both, were products of this culture and to this day I honestly believe that they loved me and thought they were acting in my best interests. They wanted me to do well and to them that meant I should study hard, be a model citizen, get into a good college and train for a career. I suppose I should consider myself lucky that neither of them was particularly religious and as a result did not push any of the many lies of religion upon me.

And so there came a point in my young life that they no longer encouraged me to write. My father no longer sat with me and my notepads and pencils and my mother seemed to have lost interest in the things I would write and enthusiastically present to her. While they still encouraged me to write they told me I should focus away from fantasy and other imaginative things and instead put work into more academic things.

I trusted my parents and though it was hard for me I tried my best to become more grown up. I worked harder at my studies and began to make plans in my head for what might lie ahead. I remember quite distinctly the time when I took my favorite notepad and my little blue-lined notebooks, along with my collection of pens and pencils, and placed them in a large shoebox. I taped the shoebox shut and put it in the closet in my bedroom. In a way I was saying goodbye to all the special things that had really made my little heart sing.

Little did I realize then that the little redheaded girl was creating the very first major spiritual blockage in her life. It was the first of many and with such acts there is always a price to be paid.

Now when my mother or father would ask me what I wanted to be when I grew up I would answer that I wanted to study law. I was somewhat interested in law but not nearly as eager about it as they might have thought I was. Still, it seemed to please them and I took some pleasure in seeing them glow with the thought that one day their daughter might become a lawyer.

Life does not always go as we want it to, especially, I think, when a person doesn't put the full weight of their desires and dreams into it. So it was with me. By the time I neared the end of high school I had begun to be quite resentful of both my parents for stifling the magic of my late childhood. And I was angry at myself for allowing it to happen. My grades faltered along with my attitude and though I still managed to graduate it was not in the glorious way my parents had hoped for.

Law school was out of the question, at least for now. I realized if I ever wanted to go to university I would need to go to a community college first in order to get my grades back up.

Yet at that time my heart was no longer a party to that dream. All I wanted to do was to wander around and see the country and perhaps to have a few adventures. Being the only child of a lower middle class family traveling to Europe or somewhere like that for a year or two was also out of the question, at least according to my parents. As I was still living with them they insisted I go and get a job and learn what they called responsibility in the world.

I gave in to their demands and went looking for a job. Eventually I found one waiting tables in a restaurant. Yes, it earned me some money and my parents, being honorable people, never asked me for one dime of what I earned. Still I volunteered to pitch in and I helped out where I could.

Serving people at the restaurant sickened me to my very soul. I had never experienced the strong emotions of loathing to the degree I experienced them when I was thrust into the position of servant. It was as though something deep in my nature had been triggered. There was arrogance there, as if somewhere deep in my soul there was a long lost ancestor, a warrior woman, standing defiant in the wind telling me not to lower myself. She was telling me I was meant for something greater.

The sudden experience of loathing and the comprehension of this warrior woman within surprised me quite a bit. Within days of this realization I was out looking for another job. This time it was working in a factory. The factory was not the nicest or safest place to work and I worried about what kinds of toxic things might be floating around in there, but it was a union job and I was told that I was lucky to get such a job at my age.

I gave away a good number of my years working in that factory. I became a part of the crowd there. For the most part I seemed to fit in with the mundane people who showed up every morning, punched a clock, and worked away like drones. I may have seemed to fit in with them but I knew in my heart that I was never really one of them. For years I convinced myself that I was simply playing a game, like I was undercover, and one day I would simply walk away when this charade had served my purposes.

In a way I was fooling myself. I gradually became used to the money and got lost in the material world. Before long I had a small car and a small loan to go along with it. I had a credit card and the debt to go along with that. I began smoking cigarettes simply because that is what the other girls at work were doing.

And of course then there was liquor. At first it was simply an occasional night out with the girls to let our hair down but then, later, as the stress in my life grew, so did my desire to drink.

And more years passed. With each year I realized I was fading further and further from the world of the little carrot-topped, freckle-faced dreamer. I was gaining weight, becoming solemn and grim about many things. It seemed that the color had faded out of everything. I saw the drinking as a friend, as a way to escape the gray hell I had become a part of.

Liquor is no friend to anyone. It might seem that it is, but it is not. In later years a wise man told me that in excess anything can be dangerous but that liquor was particularly well known for serving itself.

Just like hate. I realized that down deep inside I was beginning to hate myself. I was beginning to hate everything. I found myself wondering where the little girl who had so much love and light to spread around had gone. There were many, many times when I would just sit alone in a dark room and cry. I would cry for the lost little girl who had given away her dreams and who now found herself lost in a world full of nightmares and slaves.

Sometimes, when I was at my lowest, when I felt like there was no tomorrow and life was not worth living anymore, I could have sworn I heard a kind of thumping sound inside my head. It was like the sound someone might make if they were knocking their hand against a really thick plate glass window. It was an odd sensation, one that I felt more than heard. On those occasions I wondered about it and then, as always, set it aside as blood pumping in my ears. I shook it off, just as I shook off many other sensations. I now know they were warnings.

My father died of heart complications just a few days after my thirtieth birthday. It was sudden and very unexpected. It threw an added twist of chaos into my already swirling world.

Father's death devastated my mother and she slowly faded away. About a year and a half later she was gone too. I had no siblings to support me and I realized that those I thought were my friends were little more than surface sympathizers with no real caring for me underneath. There were good buddies to be found in abundance when there was a bottle to be passed about, but beyond that…not so much.

I was rather surprised to discover, sometime after my mother's death, that my parent's home was not owned by the bank. My father's hard work, with contributions from my mother as well, had seen the mortgage paid off in full mere months before my father's passing.

The irony of a man's life-labor coming to fruition only months before his death was not lost on me. I sold the house. There was no way I could ever live there again. I gave away or sold what I could and took a small amount of my parent's possessions to live with me in my tiny apartment. Though I now had a tidy sum in my bank account it was no real comfort. My parents had been somewhat grim in their twilight years and we had grown apart, yet they were still my parents. I would have given all that money back and more just to have more time with them.

I was lonelier than ever.

And yes, there was the bottle again, always there like a snake, luring in the unwary.

Eventually the drink nearly cost me my job, which was really the only thing I had left, pathetic though that was. In retrospect I should admit the company was kinder than it could have been. Instead of firing me for showing up to work so hung over I was still drunk, they arranged for me to see a counselor.

My co-workers all grumbled about the counseling and advised me to complain to the union. I knew that the union was responsible for me getting this second chance and I wanted to go and talk to someone. I thought perhaps if I could talk to someone who was neutral I might be able to figure out where I had gone wrong so many years ago.

Eventually I found myself sitting in an outer office, waiting for my appointed time. The counselor was a very nice, welcoming woman who was a very good listener. Within a few minutes of sitting down across from her all I did was cry and cry. The session was exhausting. I felt as though I had emptied a part of my soul on the carpet of the counselor's office that day. And yet, somehow, after taking this first step I began to think maybe there was some hope. Perhaps there was a way I might find a path out of the nightmare life I was trapped in.

On the way home I stopped at a café for a much-needed cup of coffee. In those days there were still a lot of places which allowed smoking inside. I was trying to quit that habit and I decided to sit outside beneath an awning and have my drink in the refreshing September air.

'It sounds like someone pounding their fists on thick glass, doesn't it?' came a voice from nearby.

Surprised, I turned to see an old woman sitting at a nearby table. She was quite elderly and appeared to be of First Nations heritage. I estimated she was probably well into her seventies though her long, grey hair still had a substantial amount of midnight black in it, despite the encroaching gray. I remember thinking she had probably been quite the beauty when she was a young woman.

She sat there, all bundled up in her grey and black wool jacket and smiled at me as though we had known each other for many, many years. Her eyes were a very light shade of brown, almost a honey color, and I wondered what kind of ancestry had produced such a unique coloration.

I looked around, thinking perhaps she was speaking to someone else.

'Excuse me?' was all I could think to say.

There was a very powerful aura about this elderly lady. I could feel it almost immediately once she began speaking to me. Her voice was soft and warm and somewhat deeper than one might expect from an old lady. Her presence was very calming and did not trigger the mind-your-own-business reflex I was gradually developing.

'I have been where you are, child,' she said kindly. 'You have a lot of troubles in your life and they are running you down a dead end road. I can see it written all over you because I was down that road too, years ago.'

Was I that obvious? I began to feel very embarrassed. If one old lady, a stranger, could see my problems like that, what did those closer to me see?

'The true woman-spirit is still in there, you see,' the old lady continued. 'I can see her in you as well. She is the spark inside you, the reason you are not dead yet. She has been trying to tell you that she wants to come out and help you. That's where that thumping sound comes from, sweetie, that sound of fists pounding on glass. It's the glass of this bad medicine world.'

I felt the hair running up the back of my neck standing on edge as a chill ran down my spine. How had she known about the thumping sound?

This old woman was the kind of person I wish I had known when I was a little girl. I had never known my grandparents and there were many times when I wished I had a grandmother or grandfather to tell me stories or simply to comfort me as a child. I felt tears welling yet again in my eyes as I looked pleadingly at this elderly lady, wishing she was my grandmother.

'How…how can I get well again?' I asked quietly, my voice half a sob.

The elderly lady got up and came over to where I was sitting. She set her purse down on the table and sat down next to me, placing her arm around me.

I lost it and for the second time that day I fell into a storm of grief. I cried and cried and cried, right there on that old lady's shoulder.

She was very kind and patient. She let me cry and while I did she simply patted my back and made the kind of 'there, there' sounds that any grandmother would. All this did was cause me to cry more. It was as though she knew and expected this to happen and just rode out the storm along with me.

Eventually, as I ran out of tears and calmed myself down, the lady offered me a handkerchief to dry my eyes. I gratefully accepted and returned it to her after a moment.

She looked at me with those strangely bright honey-brown eyes and asked me if I was going to be all right now. I told her I had begun to see a counselor and was feeling a tiny bit better about life as a result.

'Now, you asked me how you can get better again,' she said at last. 'Well, I'll tell you that the longer you stay in this place the more bad medicine will accumulate in your spirit, dear. The very best thing for you to do is to go away from here and heal yourself up.'

'I have no one,' I said. 'My family is gone and I have nowhere to go except here.'

The old lady looked at me very intensely for a few minutes, as if she was trying to figure something out about me or perhaps trying to make a decision. Her gaze was quite focused in that brief time and for a very small moment I began to be afraid. I felt as if perhaps this lady was far more than she appeared and that maybe behind the gentle grandmotherly surface there was something powerful and predatory.

'Has anyone ever taught you about totems or about medicine animals?' she asked at last.

I had heard something about this kind of thing years ago. I knew that in some indigenous societies the people were guided by powerful animal spirits who they looked to for help and guidance. I nodded in response to the lady's seemingly unusual question and related what I knew.

She nodded, never taking those fascinating light brown eyes off me.

Finally she said, 'Raven watches over you. It is pretty obvious when you know what to look for in a person.'

'Raven?'

'Yes, Raven. He is a trickster of sorts but also a very powerful teacher of many things,' she replied with a wistful half-smile on her face. 'He is very noble and has brought a great many good things to the world. You are lucky to have someone like that still watching over you. There are times when these watchers, these spirit people, get sick of the things we do to ourselves and leave us. When that happens a lot of the time we just give up and die.'

'I didn't die,' I said, thinking about the possibilities, the what-ifs in my life.

'No, you didn't die. Not yet anyways,' she replied. 'But if you want to heal you need to leave this city and all these hollow people behind. It's no good for you and if you aren't careful you will just fall back into the hole. That warrior woman wants to come out and help you, so let her do that. She's the one who you were supposed to become, not this shadow person I see sitting next to me.'

'I am a shadow person.' I sighed. I knew her description was accurate. I was a faded remnant of what I had hoped to become.

'I can still see you though, and there is hope in that,' the old lady said with a gentle smile. 'The only way you can get better is to go let that warrior woman out and let her guide you on the road.'

'The road?'

'Yes, the road.'

Again the lady was giving me that intense look. I felt embarrassed and somehow small beneath her gaze as if I was a mouse or something being scrutinized by a large predatory bird of some kind.

The lady reached into her bag, not the purse that she had placed on the table but a somewhat larger embroidered bag she had slung on her shoulder. From that bag she produced the most amazing long, glossy black feather. On the quill of the feather there were three gorgeous golden colored beads that sparkled in the light despite the gloomy grey of the day.

She reverently reached over and placed the feather in my hand and told me it was a gift and it would be a special charm to guide me on the road.

'You need to get out, sweetie,' she said after she handed over the feather and watched me marveling over it. 'Just like I got out of the place I was in all those years ago. You need to get out and go on the road. Find your young womanhood again, find your special place in the sun and the moon and, even more importantly, go find yourself a true family.'

'A true family?'

'Do you know what a place-marker is?'

'Like a marker in a book? A bookmark?'

'Something along those lines, yes,' she replied. 'I mean you no disrespect when I say that your parents were probably of that sort. They were here to act as your keepers until you were old enough to go out on your own. But other than that they did not really nurture you or ally themselves with you. They didn't stand with you when your natural instincts and dreams became known.'

I felt myself becoming angry at the old lady. My parents were dead. Who was she who had never even known them to be saying such things about them?

But then, seconds after the anger, the cold realization, powerful and deep in my stomach, told me that this person had seen the truth and was not afraid to tell me what she saw.

I felt like I was going to be sick.

'Don't feel bad, sweetie,' she said consolingly. 'My parents were the same. They had all the spirit knocked out of them and didn't even know how to do anything more than be my keepers when I was young.'

'Why?' I asked, meaning, Why had they been like that, acting only as place-holders and staying at arms' length, keeping me from following my heart?

'Because we are in the midst of a great war, sweetheart,' she replied. 'This is a war which has been going on for centuries and it is invisible to all but the truly awakened. On one side there is a great evil that wants to destroy everything in the world and all life along with it. On the other hand there are the ones who want to protect the sacred Earth and all of her children. A big part of the evil is the way that people have been indoctrinated over the centuries so that they believe nothing is wrong…and with each passing generation they become less and less spirited. In the end most are simply tame cattle.'

'And me…and people like me? What are we?'

'Lights in the darkness, dear,' she said. 'And the enemies of the earth don't like people like you very much, I am afraid to say. Just as they don't like creatures like me. So people like us need to go and find our own families, people who will nurture our gifts and dreams…and the special powers we each have.'

She leaned across and gently patted my hand.

'When you find the right teacher offer her or him this feather,' she replied. 'If they are the right people they will know this for what it is. Then you will really be on your way.'

'It's a raven feather, isn't it?' I asked, already knowing.

The lady smiled again. 'Yes, it is. Raven looks after me just like he does you. That's how I knew you for who you are, not for who this place has tried to turn you into.'

The sound of a car door interrupted us and I looked up to see a very handsome young man now standing beside a nearby sedan. He was the classic vision of the good looking leading man from some Hollywood movie. Dark hair, dark eyes and long black hair held in a ponytail clip over a fine looking sport jacket and slacks. He lifted his hand up in a sign of greeting and the old lady waved back.

She positively glowed upon seeing this young man and I assumed he was her grandson or some other relative.

'My ride is here, so I need to go,' the old lady said, standing up and gathering her things. After a moment she took my hand and looked deeply into my eyes.

'Let the warrior woman out,' she said. 'She will guide you in a good way.'

'I will try,' I said.

'All journeys begin with that first step,' she said. 'I know you will do okay.'

'I didn't even get your name,' I said, suddenly afraid that I would lose all contact with this amazing lady, this stranger who had in only a few moments shown me the feelings I could have in the arms of a grandmother.

Now the handsome young man was standing at the passenger side of the sedan, holding the door open for her.

'My name is Amber,' she said. 'Don't worry, I have no doubt that we will meet again some day. Just promise me you will think about taking that special journey home.'

'I will try,' I said again. 'I don't even know where to begin.'

Amber patted me on the shoulder and walked towards the smiling young man. She glanced back at me as she left the patio area and said,

'Start with that old box of journals and pencils you keep in your closet. You have a whole bunch of dreams trapped in there.'

And before I could get another word out, past my gaping, astonished expression, she got into the vehicle. The handsome young man smiled and waved at me and also got in the vehicle. Within minutes they were gone and I was left sitting next to a cup of very cold coffee wondering where my life would lead.

* * *

It took some time, but eventually I worked up the strength to take that little shoebox of dreams out of the closet. Amber had been quite correct, although I had no idea how she knew about the box. The dreams came flying out when I opened that box and emotions I had been keeping locked away for many years came out right along with them.

I cried a lot in those first days following my meeting with Amber, yet I realized these tears were different from the ones I had shed so many times before. There was something deeply therapeutic in them.

I kept seeing the counselor too, at least for the several months it took for me to put my plans into effect. Being able to speak to a neutral person really did help me on a lot of different levels. I couldn't help feeling that I would much rather have my new friend Amber to talk to about all of these things.

Six and a half months after I met Amber in that little coffee shop I stood outside the little apartment building I had called home for so many years. It took me awhile to get myself into the mental state I needed to seriously think about pulling up roots, and after that it was a matter of tying up loose ends.

I sold my small car in favor of a pickup truck with a camper-canopy in the back. And now all of my worldly possessions were sitting in the back awaiting my departure.

A few days before I was sitting in the lobby of my counselor's office waiting for my final appointment. I noticed an interesting magazine on the table and I read an article about the wildlife of the Pacific coast of British Columbia. Among the pictures I saw a photo of two huge ravens sitting in the branches of a giant cedar tree. In that moment many thoughts and ideas all exploded in my head at once.

I had been pondering where I would go. Indeed, everyone I knew, from my co-workers to my somewhat surprised boss to the manager of my apartment building, all wanted to know where I was going and what caused me to quit my job, give up my flat and cut all of my earthly ties.

At first I had no idea and this really bothered me. I even considered flipping a coin or traveling south to the United States to try and find my way, yet none of these ideas rang true with me.

And then I saw the magazine with the pictures from BC and I knew I wanted to go there. I wanted to go to a wild and free place where one might see grizzly bears and killer whales and huge black cedar-dwelling ravens, just like the one who had given Amber the beautiful feather that was now one of my most sacred possessions.

Amber had saved my life, though I knew if I ever saw her again and told her so she would just smile and say no, I had saved myself.

Thinking about her still made me grin. I had not seen her or her good-looking young male companion again while I lived in that area, though I frequented the coffee shop many times after that fateful day. I was very frustrated about this at first but then remembered her saying we would meet again one day.

And I believed her. There was something about that honey-eyed old grandmother that made me believe I would see her again, somehow, some way, some day, no matter what.

So I piled my precious shoebox of memories and a small backpack into my truck, right next to my old guitar that I had never learned to play. I waved goodbye to my kindly old former landlord and steered toward the freeway. I would go west and the warrior woman inside me would guide me on my journey.

In books and in the movies you hear about the hero who comes to town, does his thing, and then leaves, never looking back. I never really believed in that dramatic kind of thing and thought I might peek back in just to see if anything had changed…or just to be a rebel.

I certainly didn't think of myself as a hero and I certainly had had no great adventure in the place I was leaving. All I really saw drifting in my wake were the ghosts of my parents and the dreams they once had for me. But ghosts can go anywhere as long as you keep them in your heart with a good helping of loving memory.

As for the rest…I didn't look back.

2. The Shattered Mirror

I traveled the roads and highways for a good long time. I had some money and I was in no particular hurry to get to the land of the ravens. I knew I would eventually arrive where I needed to be and so I was content just to travel down the highway, stopping here or there as the desire carried me along.

I had a lot to think about during the journey. There were so many ideas and emotions I had kept bottled up in my heart over the years and it took quite a while just to process it all. I had been living a lie for so long. I was not born to serfdom, yet through the acts of my parents and by my own hand I fell right into line with the rest of the ones my teacher later referred to as *herdlings*.

Herdlings. It's a word we use in my tradition to describe the greater mass of humanity: a large herd of semi-mindless herd animals whose primary desire is to find comfort, to consume, and to reproduce. My teacher always had a somewhat sour look on his face when he used that term. He did not mean it in a pleasant way and it always seemed like it left a sour taste in his mouth.

I had come close to becoming one of them. Very, very close.

There was always a small fragment of truth that I kept close to my heart. This little bit of truth always kept watch over me so I didn't ever stray too far over the edge into the herd-world. It would poke me occasionally to remind me I didn't belong in the mundane world the way so many others did. Despite the drinking and the carrying on it is what kept me from sliding completely out of reach of my common sense, and of the warrior woman within.

Now that I recognized the warrior woman my relationship with her began to pick up a little speed. She had been buried for a very long time. She was like a seed that had never been properly allowed to germinate.

For a large part of my life I had not developed my warrior womanhood at all. I was like one of those stunted, scruffy looking little trees you see growing between cracks in the concrete or along heavily polluted highways.

The warrior woman wanted to come out and help me correct the mistakes I had made, yet she was cautious. I felt like she was telling me to go slow, to have patience and not try to rewire myself too much or too soon.

It was good advice. I know that now and I think I knew it then, but every once in a while I would find myself craving more than she was willing to dish out.

One evening when I guess I was a bit more eager than other times she suddenly stopped me in my tracks. The little dialogue I was having with her suddenly came to a halt and for a second all the chatter going on in my head came to an abrupt, screeching halt. I got the impression she was saying 'Soon, little sister. Very soon now.' Her tone seemed so stern I backed off of my impatience and my wild thoughts and left it alone.

Many regrets followed me as I drove across this almost impossibly huge country of mine. Who doesn't have regrets? I had many and I knew I had to give each of them a voice as I let them out of my memory.

I regretted not being closer to my parents most of all. When I was simply a kid it was on my parents to motivate that kind of thing but as I grew older I think I might have done more.

I also regretted not going to college. I wondered what kind of life I might have had if I tried to better myself through education. Not necessarily law school, but anything that would have kept me away from the workaday hell I eventually found myself living in.

I had many regrets about many things, yet it is not my main purpose to cover that ground here. I want to tell about my journey toward the old ways and a bit about how I got there.

I had heard people tell different stories about how long it took them to drive across Canada from one coast to another. The numbers varied but the average was a week and a half to two weeks. I never heard from anyone who had literally raced across at high speed. Canada is truly huge and as I made my way along the highways I realized that when she is seen on the map, reality does not do this country the right amount of credit.

With all of my little side trips and roundabout routes it took me the better part of a month to reach Calgary, in southern Alberta. I was taking my time and I sometimes stopped in an interesting place for a day or two. Once I stayed in a particularly beautiful place for about a week and finally had to shake myself awake again to the reality of my quest so I could get moving again.

Calgary can get very messy during the early spring and as I came in along the freeway heading west I could see that winter was finally letting go of her hold on the place and leaving a muddy mess in her wake. I decided to stop at a roadside motel for a day or two just to get my bearings and relax from the white-line fever.

I stayed there for three days. During that time I received several indications that I was on the right path. People of another age might have called them signs, but I did not yet have a term for these coincidences.

The first sign appeared one afternoon while I was walking in a small park next to a river. A lot of people were getting out to enjoy the sunny day that had appeared amidst all the grey. There were people walking with their kids and couples with their dogs. People were quite happy to get out after spending so much time indoors during the cold season.

I was sitting by myself on a bench in this park when an elderly white woman, possibly in her sixties, suddenly appeared and plopped down on the bench next to me.

She greeted me in a cordial enough way in a quaint English accent. I returned the greeting and before long we were engaged in a little chat there by the river.

She told me that she had seen me earlier down by the motel and asked if I was a visitor to the area. I told her I was and gave her a highly edited version of my tale.

She smiled and nodded politely when I was done speaking. She said that I had best not tarry too long in Calgary, because when people feel a strong call to go somewhere or do something they should listen to their hearts. She then explained to me that she had come to Canada many years ago with her husband, who had been with the Canadian Forces in Europe. She had not really ever liked southern Alberta as it was very unlike her childhood home in England, yet she had stayed here because it was her husband's hometown and he had loved it very much.

Now, she explained, her husband was gone, taken by cancer the year before. She found herself quite alone here in a city she had never really considered to be home.

'What is stopping you from returning home to England?' I asked. The words came suddenly tumbling out of my mouth without much thought and I immediately regretted them.

The old lady saw my discomfort and smiled gently. Yes, she had considered such a move over the past months but to tell the truth, though she had the means, she was afraid that everything would be different.

'It would still be England though, wouldn't it?' I asked her finally.

'Yes, I suppose it would be, underneath everything else, wouldn't it? I had never really thought of it that way before.'

The lady stood up and patted my shoulder. It startled me and when I looked in her face I saw a growing strength and determination forming there. It seemed as if some kind of new vibrant energy was flowing through her that had not been there seconds earlier.

'What is your name, dear?' she asked me.

'Carolyn,' I replied, wondering why she had asked.

'Carolyn, my name is Elizabeth, and I want to thank you. Yes indeed, why not? Why not take a chance because, by God, what is life if not a big fat chance? Indeed, England will still be England, will she not?'

I stood and faced her. 'So you are going to go back to England then?' I asked somewhat hesitantly.

Her face was now aglow with a beautiful smile. 'Yes, young Carolyn, I am going to go…home, and I thank you for helping me wake up to that. I am going to go home.'

I couldn't help but note the irony in the situation, sitting in that park chatting with a woman I barely knew. Elizabeth had made her decision to break free of the life she currently lived and travel to the place she had always thought of as home, while I had put as much distance as I could between myself and the place I had once thought of as home.

'Carolyn, you have been of great help to me in this,' Elizabeth said, taking my hands. 'I don't know why, but there is something about you, my dear, that makes me think I can fly free.'

'I am glad I could help,' I said sheepishly.

'Here, I want you to have this. A small token from a soon-to-be fellow traveler.'

With that she slipped a ring from her finger and placed it in my hand. It was bright silver and quite heavy. On the flat, oval face of the ring was a relief of a bird's head which protruded out somewhat from the background. It appeared as though the bird was in the process of leaping out of the ring. It was a truly beautiful piece and I was surprised to realize that this bird was a rather large crow.

'I can't take your ring,' I began.

'Of course you can.' She smiled. 'It is the least I can do, especially since I am flying home and you are, in your way, flying home as well.'

'I don't understand.'

Elizabeth looked at me very closely and for a second I was reminded of the scrutinizing look that Amber had given me on that September afternoon, seemingly so long ago.

'You feel like you don't have a home, love,' she said at last. 'But that is only because you haven't found your home yet. I believe that you are heading to your future home right now and when you get there you will find your beautiful family and your beautiful ravens.'

I had the urge to cry when she said that, but I managed to keep from doing it. I wondered if she was correct. Would I really find my forever family in the west where the ravens flew?

I thanked Elizabeth for her generous gift and she gave me a firm, warm hug, telling me that it was I who had given her something far more precious. With that she wished me a fond farewell and walked away. There was a very youthful spring in her step and an energy unlike what one might expect to see in an elderly Englishwoman. I knew that her old dreams had been rekindled and she now burned bright with the thought of finally going to her beloved home.

I had no idea, really, how large a part I had played in her decision but was glad to have done so. For a moment after Elizabeth went prancing away to prepare for her adventure I stood there admiring the beautiful wrought-silver ring she had given me. It was heavy and I had little doubt it was an expensive piece of jewelry.

And there was the crow, perched on the branch in the middle of the bright setting with his beak sticking out in relief from the background. Crow, it is said, is the little brother of Raven.

During my adventure in Calgary there were two signs I took to be important pointers on the road of life for me. Meeting Elizabeth was the most pleasant one. The second sign happened the very evening after I had watched Elizabeth walk away through the park, brimming with plans for her new adventure.

I walked back to my motel room feeling quite happy and glad I had been able to make a positive contribution to someone else's life. I tried on the ring Elizabeth had given me and found that it fit perfectly on my right middle finger, like it had been sized especially for me by the craftsman who had forged it.

I was feeling so good I thought I would treat myself to a meal and perhaps a single glass of beer to celebrate Elizabeth's good fortune…and my own. I had not had a cigarette or liquor of any kind since I left Ontario, and I was proud of myself, especially for saying no to the smoking. I had quit smoking a month or so before I left but it had been very hard. Yet I stuck to my guns and it was getting easier every day.

And so, seeing no harm in a little indulgence, I went over to a local tavern where I found a quiet table and ordered a nice burger platter and that single glass of dark beer. It was very enjoyable and I resisted the polite offers of more drinks from the kindly server.

I was feeling quite relaxed after my meal and was heading back to my room when sign number two appeared in the form of a young man who had spoken to me once while I was inside the tavern. He had seemed nice enough though he obviously had more than a single drink in him. I could tell by his initial banter he was hoping to find a woman to go home with him and I politely declined his thinly veiled offers. I had thought the matter done with but he appeared again as I was walking across the parking lot.

This time he was not so polite. He approached me in a friendly way but when I put up my left hand in a dismissive manner, as if to say, 'sorry now if you will excuse me,' he got angry and grabbed my arm.

I am not sure what he hoped to accomplish there in that parking lot with so many people walking around, but he did not get his chance.

The warrior woman within, good to her word, picked that moment to really manifest herself. She exploded out of me with such violent intensity I felt as though I had spun around from within.

Silver flashed and I saw my right fist swing up and smash this fellow in the side of the face with a very painful punch. No matter what you see in movies, human heads are very hard. This guy's head was no exception.

It felt like someone else was doing all of this, like I was some kind of third person observer, watching from inside my own head. It is hard to explain.

I was not finished. My leg came out as I pulled away from the man's grip. The leg swept out and caught him behind the right knee. Combined with the punch he went flying face first on the hard parking lot.

'Fucking bitch!' he yelled, obviously even more surprised than I was as he scrambled up off the ground.

The warrior woman was still not finished with him. She closed and again silver flashed. Again the right fist and the crow ring went to work, several more times, until the fist came back with speckles of red all over the shiny metal. My arm was already in intense pain, as were my knuckles, yet something deep inside of me, and now I knew who she was, just kept dishing out the punishment.

I was hitting more than one drunk man who tried to get rough with me. Somehow inside there was a part of me which was being very cool and analytical about all of this. I wasn't just beating on a stranger but in a way I was beating on every single male who had every treated me with disrespect. I think this drunk stranger represented a lot of things I had come to hate about life in general.

The fist flew again and this time it brought with it a strange sound I didn't recognize. After a moment I realized it was the sound of a grown man crying. The guy who had thought to harm me was now begging for mercy.

The warrior woman within me had finally blossomed and with a fury that really shocked me. After a brief attempt at reigning her in I gave in to the experience and let her come to full fruition.

This new Carolyn didn't want to stop dishing out what she realized she was capable of delivering. The whining for mercy simply added fuel to her hatred and she wanted to keep on hitting until the pathetic sound stopped forever. But the warrior woman reigned me in and told me to be satisfied.

Sounds of movement behind me penetrated the hollow echoing sounds of my own rage. I felt strong hands grabbing my arms and pulling me back.

It all began to clear after a moment. I began to feel sick to my stomach. I saw several truck drivers had seen the altercation and come running to rescue me and ended up rescuing the guy on the pavement instead.

After a moment the burly fellow holding me let me go. His voice was deep and calming. He told me the best thing for me to do was to get out of there and go home as quick as I could. Someone might have called the cops and in today's world, who knows? It might end up with me being charged.

Another of the men who rescued me was hauling the drunk guy to his feet. His face was streaming blood and he had a pronounced limp. The trucker seemed to have little mercy on him and was telling him to get the hell out of there before he and his buddies stomped him a little more.

'Do you need a hand or a ride home?' the kindly man who had held my arms asked.

I told him I was staying in the hotel and he said I might want to think of checking out of that place. I agreed and thanked him for his help.

'You are one hell of a fighter, little lady,' he said with a rough grin on his jolly, bearded face. 'I don't think I have ever seen a fella get his ass kicked so completely by a gal, and I don't think I ever will again. You be safe now and get goin' to wherever it is you need to go.'

I nodded and once again thanked him for coming by when he did.

With one last look at the beaten man limping across the parking lot I headed to my room. I closed the door behind me and stood there for a moment in the dark, marveling at what had just happened. I had no idea I was capable of the violence in that parking lot. It seemed like a dream. A very wild dream, but a dream nonetheless. My right hand, covered with someone else's blood, told the truth and I knew there had been no fantasy involved.

I went to the washroom and rinsed off my hands and arms. I watched as the silver crow went from scarlet back to his usual bright polished silver. It seemed that his small protruding beak had been of help when I delivered my frenzied punches.

'Thank you, little brother,' I said as I finished cleaning him up. My hand throbbed and so did my right leg and my right arm. I would be sore for a few days.

I looked up to see how the rest of Carolyn was doing after this little adventure and I realized that there was a huge, grim satisfied smile across my face. My fear was gone and there was no loathing, only satisfaction.

The warrior woman had come out. She would never again go back into hiding. It was as if I was looking at a completely different woman on the other side of the mirror glass. That woman, with a sweaty sheen of perspiration, a wild bunch of red hair plastered across her forehead and little crimson speckles of someone else's blood on her face, was grinning back at me. The old me, the one who had lived in the herd world of southern Ontario, would never have recognized this wild eyed she-wolf in the mirror. The old me would probably have been afraid of such a creature.

The image I once had of myself, of meek little Carolyn, the little girl lost, had been shattered to pieces with the fist of this warrior woman…with a little help from her crow companion.

The mirror to my grey past had finally been broken.

I had never felt so free.

3. The Road North

After a long time, my travels finally brought me to the shining Pacific Ocean. I spent a couple of weeks simply enjoying the lushness of the south coast of British Columbia. It was very beautiful there and, as I had hoped, I got to see not only ravens perched in their great cedar trees but also many other types of wild creatures in the green places, including a black bear.

I realized that the power in the land was much different from any power I had experienced before in the east. Even Calgary possessed a certain energy to it and I wondered if that place might be more beautiful in the summer when the prairie-lands were green.

Compared to the west coast, the place where I was from seemed like a dead and empty shell. I think this is due to the activities of humans and their pathological need to cut down forests, pave, put up ugly grey buildings and then bring in more and more people. I hoped that the west would never become like that though I could already see traces of it in Vancouver by the sea.

At last I found myself in a nice little community in North Vancouver and I considered the possibility that I might settle in there, at least for a while. North Vancouver has access to beaches and there are a good many hiking trails that lead into the nearby coastal mountains.

So yes, for a time at least, I thought I might settle down. I took a small apartment by the river that runs down from the mountains and spent some time exploring the area.

I took about a month to walk and explore and try to enjoy life there in that smallish little community. Yet inside of me there was this nagging little voice telling me 'Not yet, not yet. You are not there yet.' It felt like a tension in my belly that would sometimes appear stronger than at other times.

My instincts were talking to me. They had a different voice from the warrior woman within.

I had heard very little from her lately. She seemed quite happy to relax and enjoy the bit of peace I had found for myself.

One day when I was out walking I decided to stop into a local café for a cup of coffee. I went into this neat little place which was crammed with local art, a lot of it the creations of west coast Native artists, and was lucky enough to find a seat. The place was quite busy and from the sounds of the conversations around me the people in there were mostly locals.

'Mind if I cram my butt into that chair over there?' a smiling Native fellow said as he hovered nearby, steaming cup in his hand.

I smiled back and nodded, moving slightly so he could get into the out-of-the-way chair without spilling his coffee.

The place was quite tiny and full of people. I considered myself lucky to have found a seat and this young man seemed to have timed his arrival perfectly to grab a spot.

He was of average height and quite lean, with classic Native good looks and his sincere looking smile added to that. He also had straight glossy hair neatly brushed at shoulder length. A small white tooth of some kind hung on a leather thong around his neck and as he was maneuvering to sit down I noticed that his light grey sweat-jacket had a multicolored Medicine Wheel embroidered on it. Grey sweatpants and white Nike running shoes completed his ensemble. He looked as though maybe he had been out for a jog.

When he was settled into his seat he put down his cup of coffee and nodded toward me once again. 'Sometimes there are advantages to being a bit skinny.'

'I might not have been able to get into that chair myself, with my hips and all,' I said. I afforded him a smile right back because my instincts, which I had been fine tuning a lot of late, told me that this guy was not a threat of any kind.

'I'm Russell,' he said, offering his hand.

I took it and introduced myself.

And that is how the road of my destiny changed once again, or perhaps it had always been written that way and had simply been waiting for me to be in the right place at the right time.

Russell, it turned out, was a very interesting man. He exuded a kind of natural, casual energy that made me feel very at ease around him. My immediate impression was that he was a kind, good-natured person who would probably make a loyal and steadfast friend. My immediate impressions were pretty close to the mark, for as we talked that morning in the café I started to have the feeling that maybe I had met him before…maybe in another lifetime…and in that lifetime we had been friends.

Russell was a kind of jack-of-all-trades. He knew a fair bit about a lot of different things but his most passionate hobby was photography. He was polite enough to chat on other subjects but he did say if I ever wanted to know anything about the art he would be happy to fill me in.

The other thing Russell loved was flying. He was a private airplane pilot and made a living as a guide and courier. He only lived in North Van part of the year and the rest, when he wasn't working, he spent up in Pemberton and Lillooet with his family.

As Russell described the two communities I could see he had a lot of love in his heart for both. Pemberton was a smaller community, mostly rural, that lay at the base of massive mountains with rolling green spaces and wild rivers. Lillooet was geographically quite different, being somewhat more arid and settled in beside a great river running through cliffs and hillsides.

Talking about these places also got Russell talking about the friends and relations he had there. He spoke fondly of his grandmother who lived most of the time in Lillooet and of his cousins and especially of his uncle and his grandfather in Pemberton.

And throughout this, especially when he spoke about Pemberton, I felt that little tingling tension in my stomach fade a little. At first I hadn't noticed it but after a while it became fairly obvious and I paid attention. The little tingle had been there pretty much constantly ever since I began thinking of settling in North Van. Now, when I listened to Russell speak about Pemberton that little sensation began to fade away quite distinctly as though it was trying to tell me something.

'I just realized that I'm talking so much about me you aren't getting a word in edgewise,' Russell said, cutting into my thoughts. 'Sorry about that.'

I must have looked like I was bored or distracted. I told him it was perfectly okay and I rather liked hearing about his other homes. 'Tell me more about Pemberton.'

And Russell was only too eager to oblige.

The day after I met Russell in that little coffee shop I made a decision to stay where I was, at least for the time being. Interestingly enough, the little nagging tingly feeling did not return straight away as I thought it might. There was much I needed to learn in this new place and I was intrigued with Russell and the many beautiful communities that lay waiting just a few hours or so up the highway.

My extended stay in North Vancouver lasted three more months and I ran into Russell quite often at that little coffee shop. I looked forward to our conversations and hanging out with this very interesting and kind man. I realized quite early on that while I had an attraction to Russell it was not an attraction of a romantic nature. It was more like the feeling you might have towards a brother you had never met. I felt safe around Russell. I felt that he would never lie to me or take advantage of me in any way. He was a gentleman but more than that, much more…he was a warrior.

We did not exchange phone numbers or addresses. We would just run into each other in that tight-knit little neighborhood. We had an informal custom for these meetings: I would buy coffee and Russell would pay for whatever we had to eat and I would listen intently to the tales of his many adventures.

Russell never pressed me for information about myself. He was very respectful in that regard and only commented on it once, after I had apologized for not being very forthcoming about my own past when he had told me so much about himself.

'People are the keepers of their own stories,' had been his polite reply. 'Sometimes your story is not ready to be shared.'

And so we left it at that.

Russell's stories were always so rich and deep. There was an excitement to them that came from Russell's spiritual connection to the land and to the people he often ventured out with. His relations, as he called them, were sometimes blood relatives and sometimes very close friends. They always played a big part in Russell's life and he wasn't shy about speaking about them in glowing terms. He also referred to animals, fish and insects as well as trees, rocks and spirit people as his relations, so from time to time I found myself interrupting him for clarification as to which was which, or more properly, who was who.

Russell carried within himself a deep power. His energy gave me the very strong impression that when I looked at him I was only seeing the tip of the iceberg, that there was a lot more beneath the smiling face and the devil-may-care attitude than met the eye. In many ways I believed I had met him for an important reason, though I wasn't quite sure what that reason was at the time.

Time passed along as it always does. Eventually I realized I had known Russell for over three months and I had gotten to know North Vancouver and her big sister, Vancouver, across the harbor, quite a bit better.

On a sunny afternoon in July I found myself sitting on a park bench down by the sea, watching the gulls and a pack of small boys playing on the beach. Suddenly a voice I recognized called out to me and I saw Russell walking by with an older Native gentleman at his side. I waved back and went over to say hello.

The man with Russell looked to be in his late sixties perhaps. He had an iron gray head of hair that once had been as dark and glossy as Russell's. The older man's hair was longer and held back in a ponytail over the beautiful black and grey sweater he was wearing. Though the man looked fairly average in build and appearance there was something about him that almost immediately triggered warning bells inside me. These were not the kinds of warning bells that said 'get away' or 'bad person.' Instead they said something like 'very powerful person, approach with caution.'

I thought perhaps this man was an important elder in Russell's community or someone of importance from North Vancouver. He oozed power that even at a distance was very dark and earthy. There was one part of me that wanted to run as far away from him as possible, while the other side wanted to go up and give him a warm hug. It was a very interesting yet very confusing feeling, something I had never felt before in my life.

'Carolyn, I would like you to meet my grandpa,' Russell said proudly. 'It's a rare thing to see him down here so it's good timing to run into you.'

Russell's grandfather offered his hand in greeting. The grip was firm and strong just like his dark grey eyes which seemed to bore right through me for a moment before lightening somewhat.

'Hello, Carolyn,' he said, his face now bearing a gentle, friendly smile. 'Russ here tells me that you are new to the coast.'

'That I am, sir,' I replied.

The old man shook his head slightly. 'No, no, *sir* has never been a word that rings right with me. Call me Oliver.'

I spent the afternoon with Russell and his enigmatic grandfather, Oliver. We enjoyed a pleasant walk along the beach at Ambleside followed by a delicious lunch at a local restaurant and Oliver added to the tales his grandson had told me. He had originally been from the east like I was though he had come west a great many years ago. Oliver was Plains Cree, though he did not say which of the Cree communities in Manitoba he had come from. It was apparent quite early on that his heart was here in the west among the mountains and lush green forests.

'The energy here, the spirit here in this land, is amazingly powerful and not a day goes by where I am not reminded that I did the right thing in staying here in B.C.,' he said. 'It's like there is a worn-out feeling in the east. Besides, the spirit people here have much to teach.'

Oliver spoke at length about the beauty of the land and the many amazing things that could be found here. He spoke with an almost childlike glee when he recounted one or two of his own adventures 'up country,' as he put it. Though he was an elder of some sort it was fairly obvious that the spirit which inhabited his aging body was anything but old.

One of his stories involved Oliver and his best friend Emmett stealing the wheels off of government trucks that had been surveying for logging companies. Actually they had not really stolen the wheels but had removed them – from four pickup trucks – and then placed all of the wheels neatly back in the beds of each truck. But they had also taken care to make sure there were no tools around that the government men could reattach the rims with.

'We didn't want them there,' Oliver remarked with a sly look on his face. 'They knew that nobody around wanted them in there cutting down all the trees but they didn't care because we were just Indians to them. So we taught them that it was pretty difficult to move around on forest roads with no wheels.'

'I imagine they were pretty upset,' I said.

'Oh, they were.' Oliver grinned. 'We were only about ten feet from them when they got back to the truck but they didn't see us there, hidden in the bush. They were pretty pissed off.'

'These guys used to do this all the time. Kinda like they were environmental protestors before there really was an environmental movement,' Russell added.

'There are lots of stories,' Oliver said, giving me a slightly more serious look. 'Not all of them are about playing tricks though.'

He proceeded to tell me about the old traditions of the local Native populations from a town called Squamish up in the Pemberton valley. Even though these people weren't Oliver's people by blood relation or specific culture he spoke of them fondly as though they were his family regardless.

'When Emmett and I first arrived in the area we were fairly young and being young we could be a double helping of trouble from time to time. But the local folk in the community, especially in the Nations, well, they tolerated us at first, then they got to like us a bit and the rest is history.'

'I think I would like to visit that area one day,' I said at last. I had been thinking about it for a fair bit of time, ever since I had met Russell, and I thought I would let them know that.

Oliver looked over at me from across the table and nodded, his grin faded to a gentle, fatherly expression.

'You are a friend of my grandson so you are welcome in my home any time,' he said. 'If you ever want to come up and visit let Russ know and you will always have a place to stay for a while when you visit.'

I was very flattered by his offer and I thanked him.

The smile returned to his face as quickly as it had faded.

'You have a good spirit about you, Carolyn,' he replied. 'One in particular and I know that you know who I am talking about. Blackfeather's people are always welcome around my place.'

I felt a chill run down my spine though by now I should not have been surprised. I knew I had not done anything to indicate I had any connections with crows or ravens in my life. I was not even wearing the silver ring that Elizabeth had given me…yet Oliver had known.

'I will keep your offer in mind,' I said politely, trying to mask my surprise.

'You do that,' Oliver said. 'Just give me a bit of notice so my house doesn't look like a dump when you come.'

'Since when has your house ever been a dump?' Russell quipped. 'Your place is like a hundred times cleaner than my place is.'

Oliver raised his eyebrows in a theatrical manner. 'Oh, I am well aware of that, grandson. But mostly we have men as guests and not so many ladies.'

To this, and to Russell's feigned hurt look, we all had a good laugh.

Eventually the night set in and as a trio we walked back to Russell's little apartment. It turned out that Oliver had his well-worn yet equally well maintained Ford pickup truck parked right out front. He already had a bunch of boxes in the back and on the passenger seat of the vehicle.

Oliver made his respectful farewells to both Russell and I. He hugged his grandson and offered me a polite, gentlemanly shake of the hand.

'I need to be on my way if I want to make it back home in a reasonable time,' he told me. 'Pemberton is a fair drive off and the road…well, she has her moments.'

A few minutes later he was off, driving down the road, with Russell waving goodbye from the sidewalk.

'I'm surprised he just left his stuff in the back of his truck like that,' I said after the truck passed out of sight. 'Aren't you concerned that he might have had his stuff stolen out of the back there?'

Russell looked at me for a moment with a quizzical expression, then grinned. It seemed that grins and sly smiles ran in the family with both of these men.

'I pity the moron who would do something like that,' Russell replied at last. 'Maybe you noticed something…different about my grandpa? Maybe you noticed he has a certain kind of vibe about him?'

'Yes, I did, as a matter of fact,' I said.

'Then think about that for a minute and think about whether you, if you were a thief, would want to swipe stuff off of a Medicine Person.'

'He's a Medicine Man?'

'Well, that's about as close a word that I can think of to use that most people would get,' he said. 'There's a lot more to Grandpa than you might think. He's pretty powerful and dangerous too. It would be a dumb move to cross him.'

'He seems like a very nice fellow,' I said, recalling our pleasant conversation earlier in the day.

'He's a very nice guy, actually,' Russell said. 'But he is only like that to people who are worthy of nice treatment. The gentleman thing is natural to him but step on his tail and see what happens.'

'His tail?'

'My grandfather is very much like his Medicine animal, and I have a pretty good feeling you know what I'm talking about since it's obvious you know all about your own Medicine animal.'

I wondered if Russell knew about me all along as well. I began to wonder just how much more there was lurking beneath Russell, or his mysterious grandfather for that matter.

'Yeah, his tail, Raven-girl,' Russell said, smiling. 'Raven is written all over you if you know how to look for it. When we were kids we used to play guessing games to figure out what kind of animal everybody was. Then later as we learned more we realized it wasn't a matter of guessing, it was a matter of leaving yourself open to 'knowing.' Knowing is, after all, what it's all about; life and death and everything.'

If I liked Russell before I was beginning to like him even more at this point. He was most definitely 'my' kind of person and I knew he had much to teach. He had a deep wisdom that belied his years and I hoped that maybe one day he might be persuaded to teach me a thing or two. After all, I thought, I had been sent west for a reason, though I still wasn't exactly sure what that reason was.

'Your grandfather's tail,' I prompted. 'Did you mean something by that or is it just some west coast expression I don't know about yet?'

Russell turned away from the road and faced me squarely.

'Oh, that. Well, that's because of his own main animal,' Russell said. 'Can you tell what it is?'

I thought about Oliver and his mannerisms. I thought about his appearance and the way he moved, the way he spoke, but could not really nail anything down.

'If you are anything like him he is some kind of trickster,' I said finally.

'You noticed that, did you?' Russell smiled. 'Not bad for someone who isn't used to our ways. You must be a half-decent judge of character then. Grandpa is a coyote.'

Suddenly much of my experience with Oliver made sense. Now I could see it. 'A coyote, eh?'

'Yep. He's a coyote.'

'I don't think I would want to steal from him,' I said at last.

'Nope, not a good idea at all.'

4. Connections

Acouple of weeks after I met Russell and his grandfather on the beach Russell told me he would be heading up into Pemberton and if I wanted a tour he would certainly be happy to oblige me. It didn't take much to get me to say yes and a few days later there I was, sitting in the passenger side of Russell's beat-up little car, gazing with wonder at the vast mountains that served as a gateway to the Pemberton valley. It was August and in the deep summer heat the valley glowed with green.

The landscape was absolutely gorgeous and it reminded me once again that my decision to come west had been the right one. Everything here was alive and thriving. It was a considerable contrast to a rather unattractive small city such as North Vancouver. In the city everything seemed tame and controlled. Here, in the valley between the mountains, it seemed quite the opposite.

To one side of the highway, towering black and grey mountains rose up over thundering rivers and dense forest and on the other side, somewhat less rugged equally impressive mountains rolled away to the west. Before us lay the green fields of the Pemberton valley where there were many farms and quiet country homes.

We drove into Pemberton and got a coffee at a small shop there. The town was not overly large but fitted the bill as far as my expectations were concerned. It was a rural town, built to serve the farmers and ranchers who lived around there.

Russell's grandfather lived on the other side of the town. Russell offered to give me a tour before we headed out to his grandpa's place. From what I had seen I didn't think the tour would take long yet that didn't bother me at all. I was feeling mellow and taking in the sights and smells and thoroughly enjoying the peace.

As we sat with our warm beverages Russell talked more. He had come into that area for the first time when he was just a boy. He hadn't known anyone but he had made friends quickly. Eventually his urge to explore had taken him south to Vancouver and now he split his time between the big city and life in this small, peaceful community.

Suddenly, Russell looked up with an expression of interest on his face. Apparently he had seen someone he knew besides Dave, the guy behind the counter, and raised a hand in greeting. I couldn't see who he was waving at and thought it might be rude to turn around gawking, so I stayed where I was.

Russell returned his attention to me. 'I know quite a few people here, you know,' he said boyishly.

'I got that impression,' I replied

Russell looked up again. This time I could feel a presence coming up behind me. I looked up to see an older gentleman, probably about sixty years of age, walking up to our table. He was a powerfully built man, of average height, with a shock of short grayish brown hair. He was dressed in what I had come to think of as the 'uniform' of communities like this, with blue jeans, flannel shirt and checked mackinaw style jacket. Heavy work boots completed the ensemble.

'Carolyn, I'd like you to meet a good friend of mine,' Russell said. 'This is Ari.'

'How are you doing?' the man asked me by way of greeting and took my offered hand.

The experience was almost electric. This man had a presence very similar to that of Russell's grandfather, but it was somehow different in a way I couldn't really put my finger on. I instantly assumed that this fellow was also some kind of elder although he appeared to be of northern European stock. His hand was very rough, like the hands of a workman, and his grip was strong and firm. I suddenly wondered what he did for a living, and to that every ounce of my instincts were telling me he was a soldier or policeman. I did my best to conceal the effect that contact with his hand had on me and smiled along with the usual niceties.

Ari took off his mackinaw jacket and slid into the booth next to Russell. 'What brings you to Pemberton?' he asked.

For a few moments we spoke together about how I was on a bit of a personal quest to explore the west and find out a bit more about myself. Ari was very polite and said very little as I spoke. He simply watched me in a casual but interested way with those ice blue eyes of his. They were focused in polite interest yet I had the feeling that they could probably become hard and capricious given the right circumstances. I had no idea why that kind of thinking flashed across my mind, but it was there.

I also wondered if this man knew Russell's grandfather. They seemed to share a very similar tone of Earthy darkness in their presence.

When I had finished speaking about my adventures and motivations, Ari nodded politely and took a sip of his coffee.

'So what it is you have come here to learn, young raven?' he asked.

'Surely it's not to learn the business of farming. Or are you just getting the hometown show from Russ here?'

Again the all too familiar chill ran down my neck. Just like Russell's grandfather this friend had 'known' my spirit animal or 'Medicine Animal,' as Russell put it.

My more cynical inner voice informed me that by now I should probably be used to mysterious things like this happening – especially when I was in the presence of Russell or his friends or family.

'No, I didn't come here to learn about farming,' I replied at last, trying to remain cool, even keeled, and not let my surprise show.

Ari smiled and sat back in his seat slightly. 'I didn't think so,' he said. Then he turned to Russell and said, 'Did you know your uncle is looking for you? You better give him a call.'

'Okay, sure.' Russell replied. 'I do have a phone number.'

'That you seldom seem to pick up for some reason,' Ari said. 'I don't think there is an emergency or anything, but you know how he can get.'

'Yep.'

Then Ari turned his attention back to me. 'Ontario, eh?' he asked

'Sudbury, well, outside of Sudbury, actually.'

'I'm originally from around the London area. London, Ontario of course, but that was about a million years ago.'

The polite talk continued for a bit as such things usually do. It was as if his comment about my Medicine animal had been not such a big deal. Surely he had seen the reaction that vibrated through me, yet he chose to say nothing.

It bothered me that I seemed to be walking around with some pretty obvious flags proclaiming my spiritual status. Especially when, as far as I was concerned, I was not particularly overt about the matter.

'Tell me something, will you? Is my affiliation with Raven so obvious that everybody around can see it? If this is true I can't figure it out. I didn't think there was anything really advertising the fact.'

Ari leaned back in the seat and smiled. 'No, it's not overly obvious, like you set off a flare or anything like that. But to a person who knows what to look for it is fairly evident who has taken you under his wing.'

Russell had said nothing up to this point and was apparently watching the exchange with some level of amusement. Russell had informed me that his last name was Fox, or Whitefox in keeping with his native traditions. I could see the sly fox coming through yet again as he sat there smiling mischievously.

'Don't mind him. He's a telepath.' Russ grinned.

I suppose my eyes must have widened somewhat at that because Ari softened. He gave Russell a slight, stern sidelong glance and then returned his gaze to me.

'No, I am not a telepath,' he said calmly. 'I have one or two insights about things, which you get when you have been in the world as long as I have. And the reason I can see Raven in your life is because I too am watched by him.'

'I didn't know you were Native,' I said, feeling foolish the moment I said it. I had been told once that I had a very small amount of Native blood in me, on my mother's side, yet it was so small that it certainly didn't show in my physical appearance. I was embarrassed to have said that and must certainly have blushed.

'I have Native ancestors,' Ari replied. 'On my mother's side. But no, I don't walk in the Native way, at least not in the way I think you mean. The old ways of spirit are certainly not confined to the North American continent as I am sure you already know.'

'Everybody has a Medicine animal, Carolyn,' Russell added. 'Or at least most healthy people do.'

'So, you two are going out to Oliver's place then?' Ari asked, changing the subject.

We told him that yes, this was our plan. Ari looked at his watch and told us that he had been on his way somewhere when he had seen us and stopped by to visit, yet he was already somewhat late and really needed to go.

He got up and bade us farewell and told me it had been his pleasure to meet me. I told him that I was happy to have met him as well.

Before he turned to go he once again offered his hand. I took it and he shook it gently. 'You are welcome in my home if you should ever choose to visit. Russell knows the way.'

I nodded and smiled 'Thank you.'

And with that the enigmatic Ari was walking toward the door.

'Wow, that was pretty cool,' Russell said.

'What?'

'That he would say something like that after just meeting you,' Russell said. 'He is not normally like that, just inviting people to visit his home. Ari is very private and formal in a lot of ways. You must have some kind of special vibe going on for him to say that. It's an honor in his world.'

'Maybe it's because I am your friend?'

Russell chuckled. 'Yeah, well, being friends with me might be the kind of thing to make people NOT want to invite you over. Seriously though, that's pretty cool.'

'I'll keep it in mind,' I said.

* * *

We spent three days at Oliver's house at the other end of the valley. His home was a small but beautiful little two floor timber-frame set into the trees at one end of a cleared space in the pines. It was very neat and clean and it looked as though a good number of his pieces of furniture were antiques. Overall his home seemed more like a seasonal cabin than a year-round home. It seemed as though the place was not lived in overly much. Russell later explained that his grandfather spent a lot of time in the bush, maybe as much as half the year, so he was not the sort who could be considered a homebody.

Oliver was a very generous and kind host. We were fed great meals that included wild game meat and fresh greens from the garden. Oliver also had a nicely stocked cellar full of preserves and other tasty things he was only too happy to share with guests.

He had also made up a spare room at the top of the stairs especially for me. In it was a cozy little bed with a thick comforter and plump pillows and a small cedar chest of drawers. It had a view out over the back yard where Oliver kept his small chicken coop. Also visible were his fire and barbeque pit and a small home-built sauna next to a wooden work shed. Beyond that there was nothing but dense green forest rising northwest into the nearby mountains.

Oliver apologized when he showed me to my little cozy room, saying that if there was a way he could arrange for me to be downstairs near the washroom, he would. He told me he knew how important it was for ladies to have the convenience of a washroom nearby.

To that I dismissed his apology. It was no problem for me at all and I loved the room he had made up for me. I had noticed a bit of the woman's touch around the house and asked him if there was a 'Mrs. Moon' – as Oliver's last name was Moon.

Oliver said that, no, there had not been a Mrs. Moon in many years, but it was Russell's grandma who had come by to help him keep the place presentable.

'From time to time she comes by,' he said, smiling. 'She is really a big help. Otherwise there is no telling what might happen in this crazy bachelor pad.'

'Well, I could certainly get used to living in a place like this. You have a beautiful home, Oliver.'

To which Oliver replied that I was welcome any time.

During the time I spent at Oliver's house we went fishing at a local lake and horseback riding at a nearby farm where friends of Oliver's were happy to lend us horses and tack. On the third day we simply sat around the house enjoying the sounds of the environment.

Each night, Russell and his grandpa would light a fire in the stone-lined pit behind the house and we would sit on wooden benches and stumps listening to Oliver's stories. I was rather amazed to learn that Oliver was much older than I had suspected. He was in his early eighties at the time when I would easily have bet money he was far younger than that. He certainly didn't have that worn out, weakened world-weary way about him most folk that age seemed to have. Inside the body of Oliver Moon was a fun loving boy who never wanted to grow old. I could see where Russell got much of his attitude from and it was a delight to see.

On the third night around the fire Oliver began to talk about things of a less mundane nature. He spoke about certain Native traditions, the gathering of power, and the duty of all human beings to work with the balance of nature. Everything he said that night seemed directed at opening up an unseen world to me and I ate up every single word he spoke. I couldn't get enough his teachings.

I also suspected that much of what he was saying was directed at me. Russell had been in his grandfather's company for many years and it was unlikely he didn't already know about these kinds of things.

Some of what Oliver had to teach had a very deeply Native feel to it. It sounded like the kinds of things a person might expect to be practiced by Aboriginal people. Other things seemed distinctly different somehow, as though they came from very different cultures or places. Later Russell informed that as a younger man Oliver traveled extensively, wandering in parts of Europe, and he learned many things from traditional people in his travels. He utilized what worked for him and this led to his current practice being quite different from what an observer might see as purely Native in essence.

'He is almost more of a sorcerer than a Medicine person,' Russell explained, 'a man who walks closer to the darker edge of nature than most people are comfortable with. He can be dark and very unpredictable. It's part of the reason he is known as Black Coyote.'

We sat there well into the night, listening to what Russell's grandfather had to teach. Russell would occasionally disappear into the house and return with things like tea or coffee and, in a rather gentlemanly way, a blanket for me to wrap myself in.

During one of these times when Russell had gone into the house, leaving me sitting alone with Oliver, the older man looked at me and said, 'Of course this is all old news to Russ. He has known this stuff since he was small.'

'I kind of thought that what you were saying was mostly for my benefit,' I replied.

The old man's expression turned a bit more serious. 'We don't always talk about things like this with new people,' he said. 'But you know what? You are special in that way, so I am okay with talking about certain things around you.'

Again I noticed the power behind those deep gray eyes of his. Oliver seemed, from all outward appearances, to be what might be called a 'status' Indian. In other words, a person who had a clear line of Indian ancestors with no blood coming in from any other source, such as Europe, Asia, or otherwise.

Yet there was the question of his grey eyes. They were very obviously a dark steel gray and I wondered where such a coloration had occurred in his genetic line. I remarked on the color of his grandfather's eyes once, shortly after meeting Oliver for the first time, and Russell replied that his grandfather's eyes had not always been gray. According to what he had been told, Oliver's eyes had started off brown just like any other person of Native descent.

'What happened?' I asked.

'Spirits changed the color for him,' Russell said, as if it was the most natural thing in the world.

This naturally begged the question of why such a color change would be done and I asked it only to be told that Russell had no idea. His grandfather had never specified the reason and he had never thought to ask.

So there I was, looking again into those powerful deep gray eyes and wondering what kind of intervention had changed the color…and why.

'I am honored that you would feel comfortable telling me some of these things,' I replied finally. 'I find that the longer I stay here in the west the more I realize that there is a very big, deep world out there about which I know absolutely nothing.'

Oliver nodded and reached for some more wood to add to the fire. Moments later he looked up at me once again.

'You seem like a person who might not be too happy knowing that there was a big powerful world all around you and you didn't know much about it…except that it was there.'

'I would like to learn more,' I said. 'Really I would, but in a way I feel kind of wrong in wanting to know more because I am not Native.'

'Knowledge is knowledge,' he replied. 'It's what we DO with the knowledge that shows others who we really are. My ways are not all traditional in the way you refer to, yet they work for me. I have a number of what some might call 'white' practices, things I learned from others, that work for me quite well. I use them respectfully and it all works out.'

'I think I understand,' I said.

'Russ tells me that you are not working right now, that you are kind of able to make do without a job and you are free to do as you please. Is that true?'

I wondered just how much Russell had told his grandfather about me and I reluctantly nodded in affirmation to his question.

'My parents left me some money. I live on it now as well as I can so I have the freedom to travel, yes.'

Oliver told me that the reason he asked was because I seemed like the kind of person who might take to learning a few things that certain people he knew had to teach. Thus if I was interested he might be able to arrange a place for me to stay in the area.

'Despite his monkeying around all the time, Russell can be a pretty good judge of character. In your case he definitely found someone of worth and for people of worth there are always teachers to be found.'

His words caught me by surprise. I was from a place where no one trusted anyone else very much and for the most part people were just a blur in the crowd. Even in North Vancouver it was somewhat like that. People were naturally wary of newcomers and probably rightfully so. The sudden acceptance by Russell's grandfather and then by his friend Ari caught me quite off guard.

'You would offer to teach me?' I asked. 'Teach me your ways?'

Now Oliver's face transformed from a semi-serious almost professor-like look to a wide, sly, boyish smile. It was the kind of look one might wear when they had a terribly funny secret that they didn't really want to share.

'Let me ask you, Carolyn, why would you want to learn anything from an old Indian like me?'

I thought about that for a second before answering. I opened my mouth to offer a simple polite answer to his query and then surprised myself when a much larger flood of information came flying out. I told him about my childhood, my upbringing, my lost dreams, my addiction and my depression…and how I got lost in a world where I didn't belong. Finally I told him about Amber and how her wisdom sent me on my journey west. I told him about my experiences with the warrior woman within and what had happened in Calgary.

'I want to find out how I can really become the warrior woman I know I have hiding inside of me,' I said in the end. 'I want to really understand who I am, what I am here for and finally, I simply want to be free.'

Oliver sat there very patiently and listened attentively to everything I had to say. He acted as though he had been expecting me to go on about my life and didn't seem at all thrown off by the large load of information I had delivered in response to his simple question.

When I was done speaking he sat there quietly for a moment before asking me the color of the eyes of the old woman who had come to me in the coffee shop. I thought it an odd question but I told him in as much detail as I could remember how Amber had looked.

Oliver smiled in that conspiratorial way once again before returning his face to a more neutral position.

'Interesting,' was all he said.

He went back to tending the fire for a few moments and I said nothing, wondering what kind of thoughts might be going on in his head.

'Well, I wasn't suggesting I would be the one to offer you teachings,' he said, returning in a somewhat roundabout way to our earlier conversation. 'I have two grandsons and several nephews who do a fairly decent job of driving me crazy most of the time in the teaching department. No, I was thinking of someone else who shares some of that particular energy you have. Actually I was thinking of two someones in particular…if you are still interested in such a thing, of course.'

His boyish grin was infectious and I couldn't help but smile back. I was very intrigued and also, it seemed, frequently caught off guard by the things I had experienced around Russell and his kin.

'I might be interested,' I said at last.

'Okay, we'll see what we can come up with,' he said.

Russell came back to the fire bearing a cup of steaming coffee for his grandfather and himself. I still had plenty of tea in my mug and declined his offer to warm it up.

'I had to make a whole new pot of coffee, Grandpa,' he said. 'You know it would probably be a lot easier if you just got one of those coffee machines and dumped the old percolator thingie.'

'Are you kidding me? That coffee machine stuff tastes like roadkill,' Oliver said. 'Never touch the stuff.'

'Roadkill or coffee machine coffee?' I asked, innocently enough.

Both Russell and Oliver chuckled.

'You know, Russ, I am beginning to like this girl.' Oliver laughed. 'She is a bit like you and while I don't know yet if that's a good thing or a bad thing I am beginning to enjoy her attitude.'

'I'm glad, Grandpa, because I think she's pretty cool too.'

'Yeah, about that,' Oliver said in a slightly more serious tone. 'I was thinking that if she wanted she could go out and get an intro to Agnes one of these days pretty soon. Maybe you could give her a ride out there?'

Russell looked at me quizzically. 'Sure,' he said. 'I'm not back at the job for a few days yet so if you are in no rush to get back to the big stink I'll drive you over there.'

'Who is Agnes?' I asked, not having any idea who they were talking about.

'Agnes is a very interesting person,' Oliver said. 'You might find that you can start off by learning a few things from her.'

* * *

Agnes did not turn out to be anything like I expected.

The next day Russell and I again found ourselves bumping and rattling along a gravel road running beside a brisk, wild river. Neither Russell nor Oliver had gone to any great lengths to describe Agnes other than to say she was very wise and also a Raven person. In my imagination I saw an elderly Native woman living in a little cottage surrounded by wildflowers and various kinds of herbs.

In the comic books I read when I was a kid there was always a character with an idea in their head that appeared like a little cloud over the top of them. And then when their bubble is burst, someone takes a pin and pops the little cloud like it is a balloon.

That was me where Agnes was concerned.

After about half an hour of enduring the mild jiggling of Russell's car over the gravel road, and after an interesting close call with a herd of cows driven along by ranchers, we finally pulled into the driveway of a small white house behind a hand-built pole fence. The house looked solid and well kept. To one side there was another building that looked like a garage and there were several other small buildings behind it.

When we got out of the car we were greeted by a big, barking pack of dogs. Russ put his hands up in the air and yelled, 'Okay boys, you caught the big bad burglar.'

There were six dogs of various breeds, shapes and colors. The smallest was a little dachshund who leaped up and danced on his hind legs when he saw Russell. The dogs completely ignored me for the first couple of seconds, so glad were they to see Russell.

Russ was right down there with the dogs, giving each his share of attention and praise. There was no doubt in my mind that my friend was a well known character in these parts.

Eventually the dogs began to take notice of me and I let them all have their required sniffs. This examination didn't take long. They trusted Russell's judgment and accepted me as okay after a moment.

'Don't worry, they won't bite,' said a voice from off to one side. To my surprise the voice was flavored with a rich English accent.

A woman approached from behind the house, smiling. 'Though sometimes I wish they would bite Russ here…just so I could see the look on his face.'

Russell laughed off her comments and introduced her. This was Agnes, a woman of about my height and build who was pretty much the opposite of what I had imagined. She was maybe thirty at the outside, which put her within five years or so of my own age.

Interestingly enough, Agnes had the eyes I had expected to see in Russell's grandfather; a deep, dark brown. Her hair flowed straight down her back in a sunlight-golden ponytail, the kind of thick, straight honey blond that had lighter streaks in it. I had to admit her hair was astonishingly beautiful.

Otherwise Agnes was quite average in appearance. She had come out from behind the house wearing muddy boots over dusty blue jeans and a faded yellow T-shirt. There was even what appeared to be a streak of dried mud or dirt running down one of her cheeks.

Agnes took my hand in a firm grip and smiled as we shook. 'I guess it probably won't surprise you to know that Oliver called me up just the other day about you, Carolyn. You sound pretty interesting and I'm glad to know you.'

'News travels fast in small communities like this.' Russell shrugged.

About an hour later I found myself sitting in Agnes' kitchen enjoying a steaming hot cup of coffee. Russell stuck around for a bit, but then, making his excuses, had taken his leave. I think he wanted me to be able to get to know his friend without the distraction of 'a yucky boy' in the picture, as he put it.

So I sat there enjoying my beverage. The coffee Oliver brewed and praised as being so delicious I found to be simply horrible. Agnes, on the other hand, brewed the kind of coffee I was used to and I found it quite tasty.

Although Agnes' home appeared rather mundane and ordinary from the road, on the inside it was an amazing place. Framed paintings with nature scenes were hung everywhere and her walls were lined with bookshelves and cabinets. Plants grew in pots all over the place and served as a kind of mini jungle for her three tabby cats. Two very comfortable overstuffed leather chairs framed an equally comfy looking couch and a worn grandfather clock ticked away in a corner opposite the river stone fireplace. As I looked around in wonder at all of the amazing things I remember thinking to myself, 'Now this is the kind of atmosphere I would like to have one day in a home of my own.'

Agnes' home also had a very clean scent to. Over the more obvious smell of oiled wooden floors there was the scent of pine, incense and flowers. It was the kind of place that as a little girl I might have imagined to be a witch's cottage.

While Agnes' living room was dark and cozy her kitchen was an explosion of light and life. There were windows everywhere and the white and brown tiles of the floor brought more light in from outside. Her cabinets were made from some light wood and the countertops were white marble. There were even more plants in the kitchen than there were elsewhere in the house.

This was a working kitchen with a good many cooking tools and appliances. Copper pots and pans hung from a big ceiling rack overhead and a part of my fantasy was fulfilled in the quantity of drying herbs that hung everywhere.

From where I was sitting at the kitchen table I had a great view out into the back yard. Agnes explained that the space had been a solid wall when she bought the house but it didn't take her long to decide that wouldn't do. She ripped it out and replaced it with a greenhouse-like frame of double insulated glass that was more of a giant window than a wall.

Out back there was a wide green patch of lawn with a large fenced-in vegetable garden at one end. Beyond that there was a fence with a grassy field and beyond that there was a dark border of forest that began its slow climb up the shoulder of the mountain. I could also hear the contented clucking of chickens and a very small white rabbit hopped across the back lawn.

'You have a very beautiful home,' I commented when Agnes finally joined me at the kitchen table.

'You should have seen it when I bought it,' she replied, setting down a plate of cookies between us. 'It was ready to fall down, which is probably why I got it so cheap.'

For a couple of hours I chatted with Agnes. She seemed to be a very mild mannered person with a generally sunny disposition. She told me about the community and her life in Pemberton and I learned a few things I had not heard from Russell or his grandfather.

Eventually Agnes invited me to come out back with her. We talked while she gave me a tour of her little farming operation.

A fairly large flock of chickens clucked off to one side where they had a cozy home in a big clean chicken coop. The gate to the enclosure was open so that the chickens could wander the yard during the day. There was a goat wandering around there too, though I guessed he was the reason the fence around the vegetable and flower gardens was so heavy duty.

Beyond the garden was a smaller field and there, Agnes pointed out proudly, were her bees. I could see ten of those tall, square bee hive boxes with clouds of bees swarming in and out of the area. They seemed happy as much of the small field was seeded with clover and wildflowers.

'Bees are very sacred,' Agnes said as we stood there watching the bees. 'They are the greatest gift to my little farm here.'

After that Agnes showed me the building she called her shop. At one end was a little pottery studio complete with pottery wheel and kiln. On the other side was a little woodshop with a work table and a band saw. Old frames containing stained glass lined up against one window let in colored light, and opposite that, by the door, was a big old cast iron stove partly surrounded by a pile of rounded stones.

'Keeps the heat a bit longer in the winter,' Agnes explained.

Following the tour we found ourselves walking over to yet another little building in the yard. This one looked like a little work-shed of painted white siding with a cedar-shingled roof. The wooden door opened up onto a short flight of stairs leading down into some sort of root cellar. I followed Agnes down the wooden stairs and was immediately struck by the change in atmosphere. Here we were at least partly beneath the earth and the scent and energy of the whole place went from bright and summery to dark and mysterious.

The room at the bottom of the stairs was filled with racks and shelves and contained a good many jars and bottles. Preserves and root vegetables were packed into every conceivable corner and there was a rack full of dark, dusty wine bottles. Beyond that was a wooden door and Agnes went through that one as well, beckoning me to follow her.

There was a little room back there, reinforced with cinderblocks and wood paneling. It seemed a little warmer and cozy than the root cellar. There was a small round table in the middle of the room and to one side there was a large wooden cabinet. Beyond the cabinet was yet another door and I wondered just how far this little underground complex went.

Agnes lit a couple of beeswax candles that were sitting on the table and on top of the cabinet. After that she flipped off the overhead light.

'This is my little…conference room,' Agnes told me as she opened the doors of the large cabinet. It was full of glass bottles and other things I couldn't quite make out in the dim warm glow.

'I often come down here to think about things and have a little peace when my furred and feathered family is a bit too much.'

She came back to the table with a dark glass bottle and two equally dark colored stem glasses. She popped the stopper on the bottle and almost instantly the powerful scent of honey and flowers filled the air. Combined with the smell of warm beeswax this triggered a surprisingly emotional response deep within me. For a moment I scrambled, inwardly trying to make sense of it and in the end I couldn't. It was a strange but powerful, magical feeling.

Agnes placed one of the glasses in front of me and sat down at the other side of the table with her own glass. It seemed like she had somehow changed subtly though I could not exactly put my finger on what it was that had changed.

'So tell me, Carolyn,' Agnes asked at last, there in that cozy underground room. 'What do you think of my little place and all its neat little cubbyholes?'

I told her I thought it was very inspiring and I meant it. I certainly wanted to have a similar set up of my own one day.

'Russell speaks very highly of you and that tells me a lot,' she said. 'His grandfather seems to like you too and has asked me if I might teach you a few things. I was wondering what you thought about that?'

And so I told Agnes much of what I had told Oliver, though with Agnes I didn't overdo it and give out so much detail. I told her I was on a journey, that I knew that I could be so much more and I wanted to learn about my warrior woman within.

'It's not like we teach everyone who comes to us,' Agnes said at last, with a smile. 'Lots of people come through here looking to live off the land and when they hear about me they figure I am some kind of guru or something. I am not and I don't want to fuel anyone's imagination about it.'

'But...?' I asked. I sensed a hesitation in her words as she sat there, looking at me.

'But since the ravens sent you and since people I consider to be family like you I will think about what I could possibly teach you.'

Finally I smiled back and told her that when I thought about it, the entire experience since I had met Russell had been quite...weird. I had met all these cool people and seen so many things that were out of my usual sphere of things. I felt kind of like Carlos Castaneda might have felt when he started writing those books of his.

Agnes listened very politely and when I was done she took her glass and raised it.

'To your health,' she toasted and we both drank.

The wine in the glass surprised me. It was cool and flowing and tasted strongly of honey and peaches. It was probably the most delicious thing I had ever tasted in my life.

To the question which was obviously written on my face, Agnes smiled and said, 'It's a kind of mead. Made from honey and peaches and a few other things. It's a very sacred thing when it's brewed right.'

We drank again. I thought of the troubles I had had in the past with alcohol and somewhere, on a very instinctive level, I knew I would never have a problem with a brew such as this. It was too special, too magical for me to ever overdo it.

By now I was not surprised by her comment about ravens. I told Agnes that and she smiled again.

'It's not obvious to mundane people, it's just more recognizable to people who have their eyes all the way open,' she replied. 'Most people walk around with three quarters of their senses closed off. They are like tamed cattle, really. We aren't like that and I bet you aren't either.'

It did not take long for a light, pleasant warmth to spread through my body as the mead kicked in. Agnes told me the longer she aged this wine the better the flavor and the nicer the effects were.

After a moment or two longer Agnes sat back in her chair and looked at me in a slightly different way, as though she had come to some kind of decision. At first I thought she was going to get up and usher me out of the room, like she wanted to continue our tour of her little farm. Instead she simply sat there in place, looking at me.

I began to get a little uncomfortable under her gaze and she relented. Once more that kindly smile appeared for a moment.

She asked me if I had made the acquaintance of Ari and I told her I had met him in town when I had been with Russell. To this she nodded.

'He's the one who taught me...well, mostly anyway.'

'Taught you what?' I asked.

Agnes leaned forward. 'Have you been told anything about the traditions that people like me follow?'

'No,' I said. 'I was simply told that you might have a thing or two to teach me.' I grinned. 'In fact, after seeing your house, I thought you might be some kind of witch.'

Agnes laughed. 'I get that quite a bit but I am not what would be considered a witch. I do take such things as a compliment because I hold 'true witches' in great respect. So no, I am not a witch, though there are a few old christian ladies who give me a wide berth when they see me in town.' She laughed. 'I am something you probably have never heard of before.'

'What's that?' I asked, imagining that she was going to say she was part of some herbalists' or organic farmers' collective.

Agnes' face went slightly more serious. 'I'm Thornish,' she replied.

'You are right,' I said. 'I have heard of Scottish and even Cornish, but never Thornish.'

When I look back, it was in that moment I recognized I had been brought to a kind of gateway that I hadn't even known was there in the first place. It seems to me now that for a long time I had been guided, whether by my own destiny or by outside forces – likely a combination of both – to the point where I met Russell and later, the others.

'Thornish people are pagan folks who walk in a very special way. We are what could be described as earth warriors or even forest mages, I guess. Some have suggested that tribal mystics might apply too. None of these descriptions really nails it though because we have never fit into the mold that the mainstream tries to force everyone into.'

I remember staring at Agnes and I must have had a blank look on my face as I tried to make heads or tails of what she had just said. That trademark soft smile she so habitually wore crept back onto her face even though I could tell she was trying to remain serious. After a few more seconds she gave in and the smile spread.

'You should see your face right now,' she said. 'You really have no idea of what I'm talking about, do you?'

'No one told me anything,' I said. 'Really.'

Agnes shook her head slightly and I could tell she was thinking about Russell or his grandfather.

'One is a fox and the other is a coyote,' she said at last, confirming my suspicions. 'Boy, they both live up to the names, I tell ya. Well, there is only one reason I can think of that you came over here to see me, Carolyn, and that's so I can help you on the next leg of your journey…even if right at this moment you look like you just swallowed a rock.'

'Actually, I feel like someone just handed me a treasure map,' I replied as coolly as I could.

Inside my belly I felt a creeping warmth that flowed from my core and joined the tingly feeling of déjà vu that had been climbing up my back and into my head. It wasn't just the mead, it was something a lot deeper and a lot more instinctive. It was as if something clicked inside of me and just felt …right.

'Alright then,' Agnes said at last, filling our glasses up once again. 'If it's something you want to do, we will call Russell and get him to bring your stuff over here. You can stay with me, away from those crazy men, and if you want, I will teach you a few things.'

'I would really like that,' I replied.

Agnes raised her glass once more. 'To the future.'

We toasted and drank.

After all of the miles and all of the time that had passed beneath my feet over the years, I suddenly felt that I had finally come home.

5. The Hollowing

I sat on a rounded rock facing the forest and craned my neck around to watch Agnes drive away in her pickup truck. The rock I had chosen to sit on looked like it was the very top portion of a giant granite boulder with only a small bit poking out from the earth.

Agnes had agreed with me that such buried stones have a lot of power. She referred to them as Grandfathers not only in reference to their age, but also as a nod of respect to the customs of the First Nations people. There was said to be much power in huge pieces of stone such as this, though in my first moments of sitting there I wondered if my choice to sit on a big, cold chunk of mountain stone for hours on end was the wisest one.

A few minutes passed and the sound of the truck disappeared. I was all alone.

The day was a gray one and I was a considerable distance up in the hills that rose toward the mountains. I wasn't sure if the dark gray skies that loomed overhead would drench me with rain or not. There were a lot of things I wasn't sure of out there far away from anyone. I worried about things like bears, cougars, or even Agnes forgetting about me and leaving me lost in the bush, though I quickly dismissed that as silly. I knew Agnes was a woman of her word. She would come back for me at the appointed time.

I just hoped she wouldn't come back to find me in a bear's tummy.

For a while life at Agnes' place was fairly mundane. I was allowed to settle in and get used to life on that quiet little parcel of land. Before long I was participating in most aspects of farm life and even though I had been born and raised in the city, life in the green suited me very well. Agnes was very pleasant company and was always glad to answer questions regarding the farm or the chores. She taught me a lot in those first days and I gained skills that have served me well ever since.

One thing Agnes was not so open about was the tradition she was a part of. At first I wondered how I was going to learn about her ways if she was not interested in giving me detailed answers to my questions. I really liked Agnes and I respected her, so after the second day I decided to stop asking certain kinds of questions and just enjoy life on the farm. Agnes seemed to appreciate this but otherwise didn't comment on my sudden lack of curiosity. She just continued along in her usual cheerful manner.

Almost two weeks later, as we were finishing dinner in the kitchen, Agnes disappeared for a moment before returning with a bottle of her delicious and sacred mead. This bottle was such a dark green it was almost black and was about half the height of a normal wine bottle. The small bottle was obviously very old and the glass gleamed from beneath a thick coating of dust.

'This is a very special one,' she said as she came into the room.

Agnes set the bottle in the center of the table along with two small ceramic cups that shone with the iridescent glow of raku-style glaze. However, once she had done that she made no move to open the bottle. Instead she seemed to completely ignore it and asked me if I was interested in pie for dessert.

Agnes was an amazingly talented baker and I had no hesitation in saying 'yes' to pie. This time it was a blueberry pie served in a homemade crust and topped with locally made whipped cream.

I realized after a moment that the pie was a good distraction. For long moments, as I savored every bite, I almost forgot the ancient bottle sitting there on the table.

After we finished the pie, which didn't take long, out came the coffee and we relaxed for a moment, chatting about mundane things. It wasn't until we were washing the dishes that Agnes finally began to talk about her tradition.

Agnes had come to this valley from the outside, much like I had. She had come from Winnipeg and had traveled west to get away from an uncaring family and a relationship gone bad. At first she came to the valley seeking a long lost friend who she had heard was living there.

Unfortunately, Agnes discovered her friend had perished in a car accident only months earlier. She mourned her friend yet for some reason decided not to move on just yet. There was something about the place which drew her in and comforted her. Before she knew it, she had rented a place in the country and become a resident of the valley.

Eventually she was offered a chance to buy a nearby farm on a small acreage. That small place ended up being the property where we now stood washing dishes together.

Agnes told me she had been here nearly three years before she met a very kind old Indian elder with a 'wickedly funny' sense of humor. 'I was changing a flat out on some side road when along came this mysterious old guy in a pickup that was even more beat up than mine,' she said. 'He had that 'ol Johnny Cash music playing away on his car stereo as he pulled up, and when he saw what I was doing he offered to help. I've been friends with that crazy old coyote ever since.'

It was through Oliver that Agnes eventually met Ari, also originally from back east somewhere. In time Ari offered her the chance to learn about his very intriguing, almost witchy traditions.

'Seems like a thousand years ago now,' Agnes said. 'Time flies when you are having fun, I guess.'

Time flew as we washed dishes as well. Before I knew it we were back at the kitchen table with refills of coffee. The magical door Agnes was a keeper of began to open a crack and she told me a few things that intrigued me more and more.

Agnes became a part of something far wilder and more fabulous than she had ever imagined when she took Ari up on his offer. She expected to learn some bushcraft or maybe even some kind of mountain man magical workings from the old mixed blood Norwegian-Cree, something a little more exotic than the Native crafts Oliver had shown her or the common sense herbal traditions taught by Russell's grandma, Annie. However, it turned out that Ari was involved in something quite different and he wasn't going it alone. He was part of a wider circle than Agnes had realized.

'Sometimes we walk around without thinking about all the stuff that's going on peripherally to us,' Agnes said. 'Think about all the things that might be going on right under our feet as we walk along. Maybe there's an underground river down there, or a cave. We don't always think about things like that but they are still there.'

That is the way she described Ari's tradition. It was based on the idea that human beings were supposed to be the caretakers of the land and had been given the job by the ones who had helped humankind come to the world and develop. These Elder Kin, as they were called, expected that humans would maintain the balance rather than be the disruptors of everything. It was also believed that nature and all of the elements and intelligences of nature strive toward balance. As a result, Nature creates her own instruments to reestablish things that have gone awry. And so it was said that certain types of human beings were chosen to work with others of their kind to fix what was broken.

The tradition which Ari shared had been shown to him as a younger man and had been going on long before he was born. He was initiated at a time when there was a fair bit of change going on in the tradition, when there were old timers who wanted to take the tradition back into the mountains, away from the sight of modern people. Others, mainly the younger members of the tradition, wanted the old ways to become more visible so that more people could learn these ways of balance and nature. In the end, some of the initiates went back into their secret folds in the forest and disappeared while others, given the blessing of the elders to form a new lodge, took their ways forward in the hope that somehow they might be able to help the long-suffering world.

Ari and his initiated brothers brought their lodge forward and as they worked to help the world their levels of secrecy became somewhat less. Ari had eventually come to the Pemberton valley, supposedly to retire, but when he got there he too was taken by the energy of the land. Before long some of the others joined him and in certain situations they would pass along what they knew to those who were worthy.

'This assembly of forest warriors, for lack of a better term, was called the Black Talon Society,' Agnes said. 'No one seems to know for sure just how old this society actually is or exactly when it was founded but from what I have been told and what I have seen it was brought together long ago, in secret, as a kind of spiritual alliance between Indian people and people whose families came over from the north of Europe.'

'And I take it you are a member of this Black Talon Society?' I asked at last.

Agnes looked at me across the table and nodded. 'Yes,' she said. 'I am an initiated member of the society.'

'I am curious about that,' I said. 'I'd like to know more.'

'Do you remember a few minutes ago when I spoke about the things going on all around us? The peripheral things like a secret river running underground, maybe even beneath our feet? Well, that's what the Black Talon Society is. It's like a secret river that flows though the land, right beneath the feet of most people who don't even notice.'

'So the people in this society aren't following the native ways?'

'No,' Agnes replied. 'We are not. While we deeply honor the traditional people of these lands and are always open to their counsel we aren't copycat Indians. The tradition isn't like that. We have our own unique ways even though we have had brothers and sisters who are native and white alike. The Black Talon Society is color blind, so to speak. We look at a person's spirit, not their color or culture of origin.'

'I would love to learn about this society of yours,' I said. 'Russell was right. It is something I would be interested in.'

Agnes was silent for a moment and once again it seemed like she was considering something deeply. Finally she said, 'If you really want to learn then I think you are someone we can trust to know a few things. I will tell you that I have been keeping a close eye on you these past few weeks because not everyone who comes around is worthy of knowing what we know. But you have a good heart and a good spirit…and Russell vouches for you.'

She said that last part with the faintest of smiles. 'So I will ask you three little questions and we will see what you have to say to them.'

Suddenly I felt tense all over. I was reminded of my days in high school where we had gotten seated in class only to have the teacher tell us there would be a pop quiz.

The first question Agnes asked me was if I believed in the reality of the spirit world. She told me she wanted to know what I thought of that possibility and the possibility that there are other worlds besides our own.

From the many conversations we had already had during my stay I thought my orientation as a spiritual person was fairly obvious. Yet there seemed to be some formality to the questions and I guessed there was a traditional reason for her query.

I told Agnes that yes, I absolutely, without a doubt, believed in the spirit world and in the existence of other realms besides our own. I had never had any serious doubt of that, despite the attempts of my parents and others to get me to 'grow up.'

Agnes seemed satisfied with that answer and went on to the next question. She wanted to know if I thought there were any rules or laws in the worlds we inhabited.

I thought about that for a moment and quickly concluded she wasn't asking me to go on about the laws of physics I had learned in high school science or anything so mundane as the law-of-the-land. I told her I thought the only real laws out there, the ones that really counted for anything, were the laws of nature. I thought maybe I had oversimplified that answer and considered adding to it, but it seemed that the answer was acceptable to Agnes.

Finally she asked me, 'What do you think the purpose of human beings actually is?'

Now there was a question I had pondered myself over the years. I came to the conclusion that because humans were different in so many ways from a lot of other animals on the planet, that had to mean something. I thought it must be because nature needed gardeners and protectors to help her with her work. Otherwise it was unlikely that human beings would have developed to the extent that we had.

I told Agnes this and she nodded her head once again.

'That's very good, Carolyn,' she said after a moment. 'I kind of figured you might have those answers, which is why I am thinking about teaching you.' She paused again before saying, 'Okay, I have one more question for you and I would like you to take your time before answering it.'

And Agnes asked the final question.

I will not relate the question because later in the evening, as Agnes discussed other things, I was asked not to reveal the question to anyone else. I was told that the traditions she held sometimes had secrets and that in order to hold power some things must be kept and rarely shared.

And I agreed to that. I understood the reasoning behind her request and I honor it as well.

I gave Agnes the best answer I could to the unexpected question. It was not a question I felt could be asked or answered lightly. I did not think it was a question that could be answered in any one single way but instead would be relative to the person answering the question.

When I was done speaking Agnes smiled that warm, welcoming smile and briefly patted my hand.

'I have a grandmother in England who is something of a cottage witch,' she said. 'Nothing fancy but she is the go-to gal in her local town for people who want herbs or gardening advice or even help with their personal lives. She is well liked in her community, even by most of the church goers. Anyway, she taught me a long time ago that many things in nature are set up in sacred patterns and the star or pentacle is a useful shape to use. There are five points in a pentacle just like there are five points in many things.'

'That makes sense to me,' I said.

'So in my own case, this little session comes in five parts,' she said. 'The questions are traditional ones we use and the next thing is as well.

I like sacred geometry and I am always seeing symbolism in things like that, which is why I explained the star shape to you. Often I remember things better when I assign a pattern or shape to them in my head.'

'And the fifth thing is?' I asked.

Agnes smiled again and sat back in her chair. 'I have already been told I can teach you our ways if I see fit. I have to ask you then, what is the teaching worth to you? What could you trade for what I have to give?'

I thought about that for a bit. I knew she was not asking for money and it didn't take me very long to realize she was requesting something symbolic, a token of my desire to learn.

I immediately thought about the ring Elizabeth had given me. It seemed such a long time ago back in Calgary, but almost as soon as the thought came to me something inside me rejected it as not being a good idea. My mind flashed around a moment before settling on something that might be appropriate. I took from around my neck a small jade 'luck' ring on a silver chain. This was a small, flat, blue-green disc of the sacred stone that was not much larger around than a bottle cap. It had a hole in the center and through that the silver chain was looped. I had fallen in love with this thing the moment I saw it in a tiny shop in Vancouver's Chinatown district. The lady who sold it to me told me that jade brings luck.

Somehow it seemed right to give this over as a token of trust and willingness to learn and though I was loathe to part with it, the timing seemed right.

I handed the small gift over to Agnes and her face absolutely lit up. At first I thought this was because she admired the polished jade ring on its silver chain. However, though I could tell she found the thing pretty, it was not the reason for her expression.

Agnes seemed barely able to contain herself her voice was calm.

'Very well, Carolyn, daughter of Ellen. I accept this gift for the symbol it is. Thank you, and yes, I will teach you.'

She held out her hand and I took it. She held my hand for a moment in all earnestness before saying at last, 'I have never officially had a student before, did you know that? Of course you wouldn't know that, but it's true. I will do my best to teach you what I know.'

'I will do my best to learn,' I said sincerely.

'So to that end I should tell you my lineage since it is important in the tradition. I am Ciarán Shannonsdottir. I am the student of Raven, whose teachers were Joseph White Horse, Agnarr the Bear, and Augustus, son of Ölm. I am a member of the Black Talon Society and a member of the Raven Lodge.'

'As you know I am Carolyn Ellensdottir of many places, come to learn from the Lady Ciarán Shannonsdottir,' I said, falling into the spirit of things.

Agnes nodded very formally.

'If you wish to refer to a female Shar you may use the term 'Shaara.' It is one of the terms we use to refer to an initiated woman. Thus I am Shaara Ciarán.'

'There is no term for a male Shar?' I asked, curious.

Agnes made a humorous kind of snort, which she caught herself doing and in light of the formality of the situation, stopped.

'No, they are just Shar,' she replied. 'In fact, you will discover that us girls get quite a few of the goodies that the menfolk don't get. It's in deference to our power as females. The tradition is very balanced yet it recognizes and respects women unlike anything I had ever seen before I came to the Lodge.'

'That is very good to know.'

'However, I will tell you this,' Agnes said, once again with a sense of deep formality. 'The word Shar is reserved only for members of the

Black Talon Society. The Black Talon Society is an elite gathering of those folk who have come to walk in the Thornish way. A person could possibly become Thornish on their own, from learning from one of us or from learning our ways in some way or another, but unless they are initiated by one of us, from a Shar Master or a Shar Elder, they will never be a member of the Black Talon Society and may never refer to themselves as Shar.'

'I see,' I said, inwardly chiding myself for assuming when I should have been listening.

'The word Shar is very sacred to us,' Agnes said softly, reverently. I could see tears building up in the corner of her eyes with the emotion of what she was saying. 'It is a word which came to us from the spirit world and also from the sacred Dark Lady. It has multiple meanings to us but its deepest meaning is that of the implement of the sacred balance. To carry that term is a huge responsibility.'

I nodded, trying to imagine how deeply Agnes had connected with the Thornish ways and with the traditions she held. I realized that much of this was subjective and I would never really understand unless I walked a road similar to her own.

'There have been very few women in the tradition to date,' she added. 'With the coming of the Raven Lodge this has begun to change.'

I asked why and she simply shrugged her shoulders. 'Times have changed. More and more women are seeking something more. The old ways are coming back and more men are once more recognizing the sacred powers of us girls.'

Agnes paused for a moment before going on. 'Once you have had your Deepening we will see about getting you a Lodge-Name,' she added.

'A Deepening?'

'It is a form of sacred retreat, an ordeal and ritual that all of us do to find the deeper paths within ourselves. Don't worry, you have some training to do before you are ready for that.'

I nodded, then recalled something I was curious about earlier but had not yet asked.

'Agnes,' I said, 'would you mind explaining that look you had a few minutes back? When I gave you my necklace? I'm curious.'

In answer Agnes reached into her shirt and pulled from between her breasts a beautiful light blue stone, disc-like and highly polished, hanging from what looked to be a deer-hide thong. The stone was absolutely gorgeous and glowed in the light. Tiny colorations and patterns swirled across its smooth surface as it hung there before my eyes.

'That's why I had the look,' she said. 'There are no such things as coincidences and all your jade gift made me think of is how right you are to learn.'

'It's beautiful,' I remarked.

'It's lapis,' she said. 'It's what we call a Lore-Stone. It symbolizes the circle of the sacred balance and the laws of the multiverse. It also symbolizes the sacredness of the clan and the tribe, the magic of the Lodge.'

'A Lore-Stone?'

Agnes nodded. 'Yep. Everyone in my tradition has one. We make them as a part of our learning and we try to either make one for ourselves, or if we are not artistically inclined, have one made or even acquire one in a special way. The fact that you handed over a jade stone that looks so much like a Lore-Stone kind of caught me off guard.'

Agnes then removed the stopper from that little blackened bottle in the middle of the table. The rich, floral honey scent filled the air much like that afternoon in the root cellar, and I was once again impressed with the power of this simple beverage. She poured two small glasses and handed me one.

'Now be careful with this one,' she said. 'It is not quite the same as the one you sampled before in the cellar. It has been sung over and it is a very sacred brew.'

I took a small tentative sip. The rich flavor of cherries and honey almost overwhelmed me. It was smoother than silk and went down in a way I can barely describe. This was possibly one of the most delicious things I had ever experienced in my life.

Agnes raised a glass to me and said, 'You first lesson will be this. Among us we have a saying we often use as a toast: *May there always be steel upon the stones.*'

I didn't ask, right then, the significance of those words. I simply raised my glass and toasted with her.

'And when you are ready, come on into the living room. We will discuss the various things that may bring you into the Thornish ways.'

* * *

Four days after that special night in Agnes' kitchen I found myself out in the forest, at the base of the hills, beneath a threatening sky. I was wearing my usual uniform of the day which consisted of blue jeans, boots and a light shirt. My hair was tied back in a ponytail. Also, at Agnes' insistence, I had brought along a light wool jacket with a hood.

Agnes had told me that for this ritual it was important to have a place of shelter for the senses and that most people chose either a hooded robe or a hooded jacket for that purpose. 'Besides,' she remarked, 'It looks like it might rain and I don't think you want to get completely soaked.'

And so there I was, alone in that quiet place, preparing to perform what Agnes called a Hollowing.

A Hollowing is kind of like a cleansing diet for the soul. It is a process in which a person goes out to a natural, quiet place and attempts to completely open up to the natural world around them. The idea is to let go and try to clean out all of the bad thoughts, memories and other poisons of the modern world and at the same time try to pin down exactly where one fits into the greater scheme of things.

I was told to do two things prior to his experience. The first was to learn or rather, re-learn, how to meditate and in this Agnes was a great help. We spent hours in her living room practicing and eventually I had been able to get to a place where at least the noise in my head was quieting down.

The second thing I had to do was acquire a Lore-Stone of my own so I could take it with me on the first ritual sit.

At first I wanted to go into town and see if I could find something that would work, but somehow just going out and buying something didn't seem right. Agnes told me there were few rules regarding the Lore-Stone, except that it had to be made of a natural material and acquired with what she called 'goodly intent.' And so with that in mind I pondered and wandered trying to figure out where I would come upon such a thing. Eventually I started going on long walks on the nearby trails to quiet my mind and think about the path ahead of me.

After awhile I began to get frustrated. I was beginning to think that the only thing holding me back from getting on with the rest of the teachings was the acquisition of this small bit of rock with a hole in it. I realized I was becoming impatient and I used my walks to calm down and try to see the bigger picture.

At last I thought I had it figured out. I was walking the trails one day and found myself down by the river. As I was sitting there I began thinking about the beautiful pottery work Agnes did and of the many beautiful glazes she applied to her pots. I thought, why not make a Lore-Stone out of clay and then fire it with a beautiful glaze? Wouldn't that work? I resolved to head back to the house right away and ask Agnes if this would be something I could do.

I got up from the log I was sitting on and noticed one of my boot laces was untied. As I reached down to tie it up I realized, with a shock, that right in front of me on the gravel was an almost perfectly rounded black river stone with a nice hole in the middle!

A mild feeling of adrenalin surged through me and I realized right then that there was powerful magic already at work in my life.

I picked up the stone and examined it. It wasn't quite perfectly round but it was flat and disc shaped and had a perfect hole worn right through it by many years of being immersed in running water. It was a gift from nature to help me on my way. It was perfect.

I remembered what Agnes had already taught me about the nature of the multiverse—that everything was alive in nature, and everything in nature was sacred. So I sat there for a while with that dark black stone in my cupped palms, trying to get a feel for it and what it wanted. I spoke to it and told it about my plans and I asked it if it would like to come along with me and be my companion as I learned this new way.

I got the impression that the little stone thought it would be perfectly okay to accompany me. In return I took something from my pocket: a little bag of seeds, mugwort and tobacco mixed together, along with three copper pennies. These I offered to the place in the dirt where I had found the little rock. It was my offering, one that would not only please the spirit of the rock, but also the other spirits and creatures that lived around that place. In the way I was learning it was exceptionally important to always be polite, always ask permission and always leave an offering. Balance was very sacred in the way that Agnes was teaching me and I was working hard to become a good student.

I was very excited to bring the little stone back to show Agnes. She agreed it was a very good find and soon got me a nice piece of red deerskin cord to string it on. In a moment more she hung the stone around my neck.

'Red and black are Thornish colors,' she said happily. 'The black represents the Elder Knowledge of the multiverse and the Great Essence that all life comes from. The red represents life and fire and spirit. It's a good combination, my friend.'

And so I had become, with that simple act, what the Thornish people call a Learner. A Learner is a person who is at the very beginning of the trail to the Thornwood, a person who has been found acceptable as a student but who has yet to perform any of the various rituals of learning in the tradition.

'The way of the Thornwood is the way of the Thornish people,' Agnes taught me. 'The main body of Thornish culture is not particularly a secret. Thus anyone who learns of our ways can, if they choose to apply themselves, become Thornish. However, in order to go deeper one must participate in the rituals and become Shar. A Shar is a sacred implement and that's what we strive to be. When you become Shar you can go even deeper, cross over and become something far greater. It is then that a person becomes a member of the Black Talon Society.'

Thus I found myself sitting there in the rising breeze, thinking that this was but the first of many rituals….and worried about bears while at the same time trying to re-focus myself on the task at hand.

I sat there in that place for what seemed like days, though in my logical mind I knew I had only been there an hour or two. I was tempted to dig into my bag for my watch but staunchly refused to do so. I also wondered, from time to time, how Agnes would know when I was done. I wondered how she would be aware of my situation and pondered that perhaps she might not have gone too far and was possibly, even now, watching me from among the trees.

That did not seem to be Agnes' style, however. I had grown to know her well enough to realize it was unlikely she would do such a thing. Despite her protestations, I could never quite shake my belief that Agnes really was a witch of some kind. Perhaps she had powers I had not thought of…and at this I became even more excited in the hope that one day she might teach me how to do such things.

And then I realized that once again my inner dialogue had gone from a quiet murmur to a dull roar—and once again my head was full of chaos and loudness.

I forced myself back into the breathing exercises I had been taught. Count to nine, in though the nose, out though the mouth, focus only on the stillness and the breath…

At last I forced the inner voices and thoughts down. I took notice of these intrusions, yes, but I also set them aside and continued with the breathing. Count to nine and start over again in slow measured breaths…

It seemed to me that I had already caught myself wandering in thought too many times and was tempted to get harsh with what I saw as a sore lack of discipline. Yet I remembered Agnes had taught that these techniques were thought of as a mossy stack of deep green stones, skills that we built up so that we could master ourselves and have a clear mind. To force was to be disruptive. I had to be controlled but calm.

So I set the intrusive thoughts and images and sounds aside and each time went back to the still place I was building for myself in my heart.

At last, when I felt myself ready, I pulled the dark hood down over my face, bowed my head forward and tried to drift deeper into the inner silence.

Many things came to me in that state. Many things I had not expected and I found that the calmer I became, the more at peace I was, and the more things came out and drifted around. These weren't like the intrusive thoughts and head-noise. These things seemed to come from a deeper place inside me. They were more emotions than specific thoughts or images.

In this silent, dark space, as I sank deeper and deeper, I began to examine my life in detail. It was as if I was an outside observer, separate and integrated at the same time. I felt many emotions but as I examined who I was and what I was doing here on Earth, I became very sad. I wondered why I had not done more and I wondered why I had wasted so much of my life in a confused daze. It was the wasted years that really got to me and I began to feel wave after wave of sorrow. I tried to brighten things up and gravitate towards lighter, nicer, happier emotions, but it was as though the sorrow needed to work itself out of me.

I let go and rode the wave of sorrow. I saw my parents in brief flashes and I missed them so very terribly. I saw the friends I had held close as young girl but had let go over time and space and I deeply regretted that. I saw so many things inside that silent place, things that made me sad and regretful. At last I began to move toward the earth, the soil and the reason I had been brought here. I saw the many bad and terrible things that humankind has done to the earth and I felt deeply ashamed and afraid.

How could I allow my people, other human beings, to do this? I was human and so I was also responsible. I felt deep humility and embarrassment as the waves of black deeds washed over me. I felt the loving presence of the earth mother, our once green and fertile home, and I thought about how we were killing her. It was like stealing from a kindly old grandmother and then beating her in an alleyway behind her house.

I felt rage and horror at these thoughts and, above all, a fathomless sorrow that caused me to cry until I felt I couldn't cry any more.

And suddenly I realized I was wet. I was wet not only where tears had been flowing by the gallon, I was wet all over. I opened my eyes and realized I was bowed over toward the earth and all around me it was raining.

I blinked and looked up. I cautiously peered out of the hood and as I went to straighten my back I realized I must have been in that bowed over position for a considerable amount of time. My back ached and I thought I might end up spending time in a hot bath later to straighten it out.

I also realized that a lot more time had passed than I originally thought. The sky was darker and I knew it was quite late in the day. Finally I gave in to the curiosity I had fought off and I dug my watch out of the small backpack I had brought along.

Amazingly, six hours had passed since I watched Agnes walk away toward the trail. It was well after the dinner hour and even though it was still summer the days had begun to grow dark earlier. I did not want to be caught out in the woods after dark.

The rain began to thunder down even harder and I slowly staggered to my feet. I felt thoroughly hollowed out, exhausted on many levels, and I was very sore from sitting on the cold stone for so long. Yet I also felt incredibly clean standing there in the rain. I reveled in it and the feeling of the rain took my mind away from the many other hurts.

I took the time to set out an offering to that place before I left there. I left an apple and a small palm-full of the sacred tobacco/mugwort mix. I laid my hand on that big, mostly buried boulder I had been seated on for so long. I felt the cool of the stone beneath my hand and I offered my sincerest thanks that it had allowed me to stay there for my ritual.

At last I straightened up my sore and creaking back, shouldered my pack, and slowly made my way toward the trail. Half an hour later in a rain that had not let up, soaking wet and weary, I was glad to see Agnes sitting there in her truck at the side of the road, smiling.

'What took you so long?' she asked good-naturedly, yet I knew full well that she understood exactly what I had just been though.

As I clambered into the cab of the truck she welcomed me with a pat on the shoulder. 'I don't want to hear about any of your experience just now, Carolyn,' she said as we pulled back onto the road. 'Let it settle for awhile inside you and later, contemplate the meaning of what you were shown. The Hollowing is a deeply personal thing and you may choose to never talk about it.'

'I understand,' I said, thinking back on the swirl of emotions I had experienced back there in that little clearing on the rock. Perhaps she was right.

We swung north off the side road not long afterwards and before long were on the main road back towards Agnes' house.

'I think that you have a hot date with a tub full of suds,' Agnes said with a smile.

'Yes indeed,' I agreed quietly. 'I will definitely do that.'

6. In the Halls of Silence

We stood once more in that small room at the end of the wine cellar, the room with the small rounded wooden table in the middle of it. I recalled fondly that first day when Agnes had shown me around the farm and eventually we came to this place and sampled her amazing mead.

That first time had been a courtesy and also reflected how proud Agnes was of her little farm. She mentioned once or twice that one of the reasons she got such a good deal on the house and property was that it had been what the previous owner called a 'fixer-upper.'

'Boy was he ever not kidding about that,' Agnes commented. 'It was a fixer-upper that took me the better part of six months to make habitable.'

I discovered that Agnes' version of what was habitable was a far cry better than what most folks around these parts considered habitable. She could be quite fastidious and told me a number of tales about how she ripped out walls here and re-built this or that. It was her artist's nature and her attention to detail, not to mention the need for sacred symbolism, that made her home a magical place.

And now, once again, we walked down into that dim yet warm-feeling place beneath the ground. This time we came with a ritual in mind. Agnes had a blanket in her hand as well as a large square pillow from the living room. These she set down on the table in the center of the room.

It had been several days since my Hollowing ritual out in the hills and I did not go out of my way to relate much of what happened to me there. Agnes liked it that way and, as she told me, it was important that I keep the power of the experience to myself as much as I felt comfortable. I took a fair bit of time to meditate on what happened to me and tried to process the deep understandings I had gotten from the experience. I also spent some time smoothing out my little Lore-Stone so it had a slightly more balanced look.

One night after dinner we sat with coffee. It seemed that during these times Agnes was a lot more likely to teach me about something potent in nature. My friend and teacher told me about another step she would like me to take.

'You remember my little room next to the wine cellar, which I showed you when you first came here?'

I told her I remembered it well and thought it was a neat little space.

'Well, I call that the Barrows room,' she said. 'That name came to me when I discovered it. It was once an extension of the wine and root cellar but the minute I laid eyes on it the name and its real purpose came to me. As you probably know, barrow is a word they use in the old country for a burial mound. To me this is a deeply sacred thing.'

She proceeded to tell me how in ancient times many cultures buried their dead in large mounds that were often constructed over stone houses or structures as homes for the dead. Sometimes many generations of people would be placed in these mounds and it was considered to be a powerful act to sit or sleep on the mounds, or to hold ceremonies designed to honor—or even communicate—with the dead.

'It wasn't until the Christian beliefs started infecting everything that such places were thought of as dark or scary, yet nothing could be further from the truth,' Agnes said. 'These places were very sacred and still are very sacred to many people. Not only were they built in Europe and Asia but in a lot of other places too, including North and South America.'

Death, Agnes said, was a sacred doorway and when a person died it was only their body, here, in the Middle–World (as she often termed it) that stopped functioning. In Thornish belief the body was simply a conveyance our spirits used to experience life on this plane of existence. When the body died the spirit simply moved on to another place, a place where communication and transfer of energies could still take place when the proper means were used.

'So this is one of the reasons I call this the Barrows room,' she said. 'It's not a burial mound, though one day I would really like to see a true Thornish one built somewhere. But it's built under the earth and has that sacred feel to it.'

I told her it certainly made me feel better hearing that. 'I wouldn't want to find out this is where the students who didn't make it ended up,' I said, only half joking.

'No,' Agnes said with a grin. 'It is a place of spirit but not that kind of spirit. And it's a place where I have learned some pretty astonishing things about myself and about the workings of the spirit world.'

Agnes got up from her place at the kitchen table and motioned me to follow her into the living room. She invited me to sit down on the overstuffed couch and I did so, setting my coffee cup down next to hers on the well-worn coffee table.

I was impressed with the amazing amount of work Agnes had put into making an old beat-up farm house a very special, magical retreat. She went to great effort to bring in good quality natural materials for her renovations over the years and the place simply vibrated with safety, comfort and welcoming spirit. Many wonderful things adorned her home like little statues of gods and goddesses and even Buddhas everywhere among the paintings and ceramic pots. Combined with the jungle of plants which grew everywhere, going into various rooms – especially the living room – was like venturing into some forgotten Aztec city where treasures were lying all over the place.

In the midst of the living room was a polished wooden box that looked like a rectangular sea-chest standing up. It was made of some kind of lacquered yellow-brown wood that had been charred. I noticed it sitting beside the fireplace on the stone hearth when I first entered that room, but out of respect I never asked Agnes about it.

Now Agnes walked over to the box and knelt down in front of it. It wasn't a sea chest at all but a kind of shrine which had two doors that swung open in the front.

When the doors were open Agnes took a match and lit two small candles in red glass holders, which she placed in front of the box. Then she stepped away so I could see what was inside.

In the box, elevated on a little wooden pedestal, was a beautiful sculpture of a shrouded female figure that had a deep hood pulled down over her face. The sculpture reminded me of marble carvings from ancient Greece or Rome like you might see in a museum.

This figure had a grace and flow to it, yet there was a kind of roughness to it as well, a kind of primal-ness. In one hand the lady held a book and in the other, point down, a very short-shafted spear. The sculpture was made from some kind of stone or ceramic. It was deepest midnight black which was set off very well by the flickering glow of the little red candles.

Agnes took a small pot full of little purple flowers from a side table and set it down next to the shrine before returning to join me on the couch.

'Öndia Vé is one term we use to describe this,' she said softly. 'You will discover that in the Thornish way there are a lot of terms we have created over the years to describe things that are uniquely ours.'

'Öndia Vé?' I asked.

'One of her many manifestations,' Agnes replied. 'She has so many. I believe that there is but one Dark Lady, so to speak, and she has had an intimate relationship with human beings for many, many millennia. Different cultures have given her different faces and symbology but the Lady remains the same. The Thornish words Öndia Vé refer to a feminization of the word Önd. Önd is said to be one of the gifts bestowed upon humankind by Odin in the old Nordic tales. Önd is the breath of life and conscious existence. Vé is another Germanic word and it refers to a sacred enclosure such as an outdoor shrine. Thus Öndia Vé is the sacred energy of the shrine. We see the Dark Lady as that.'

'The Dark Mother?' I asked. Agnes had spoken about her before. The Dark Mother, also known as the Dark Lady, was seen by Thornish folk as being the primal mother, a being of unknowable antiquity who was not only one of the first sparks to come out of the primordial void, but also the guardian of both life and death.

To Thornish people the Dark Mother isn't truly a goddess. Thornish folk have little use for such terms, I was told. Instead they have another way of seeing things and these ancient beings, that some refer to as gods or goddesses are seen as Elder Kin. Elder Kin are not omniscient beings but far, far older beings that inhabited the multiverse long before the existence of humankind. Some of them, it was said, played a hand in the creation of human beings as we are today and others, taking an interest in us, have guided our species from time to time.

At the core of Thornish belief is animism, and a hard animism it is too, for the Shar, the people of the Thornwood, believe that everything in the natural world has a spirit. I was told that other things in the human world like machines and similar man-made things might also have or acquire spiritual energies of their own. In the Thornish worldview everything is alive.

The folk of the Thornwood are not goddess worshipers. The Dark Mother is most certainly not at the head of some imagined pantheon. However, she is seen as being one of the most ancient of the Old Ones and worthy of deep respect.

When Agnes spoke about the Dark Mother she spoke with respect and reverence, almost as though she was speaking about her own mother, yet with a far deeper dimension I couldn't really fathom at the time.

'Yes,' Agnes said in reply. 'The Dark Mother is the keeper of many keys to an even greater number of doors. She is the warder of the Black Root of knowledge that we humans have largely forgotten. An Irish friend of mine calls her the Morrigan or Great Queen. She is an Elder of the black Earth, of fertility, of power, of war and indeed of the deepest peace; the peace of death and the sacred cycle as it begins anew.'

I gazed on the lines of the sculpture in the little shrine for awhile, admiring her beauty. I wondered who had sculpted her.

'She is the mistress of Barrow Hall,' Agnes said after a few more moments. 'This is one of the reasons why I call that little wine cellar room the Barrow room. It is in honor of her and the essence of her. She is the elder and the seer, the wise one who wards over the gateways.'

'What you mean by gateways?'

'Gateways are passages and portals,' Agnes replied. 'Doorways from this shallow part of the great river we consider to be reality and on into the much deeper places. The passageway to the land of the spirit people is one and the gateway where our spirits go when our bodies die is another. When a spirit comes freshly to this world, when a baby is born, that's another type of gateway. There are lots of these gateways.'

'Is the Dark Lady the only gatekeeper?' I asked.

'No,' Agnes said. 'In Thornish belief there are many others. Some ward over smaller gates and some over more important ones.'

'Like life and death?'

'Yes. These things are incredibly sacred.'

'And you are a kind of gatekeeper too, aren't you?' I asked at last.

Agnes smiled. 'All teachers are, in a way, though what we do is quite a small thing compared to persons like the Great Dark Mother. She is quite literally a piece of the Great Essence that is showing itself in our worlds.'

I asked about the Great Essence and she explained to me that in Thornish belief the Great Essence was, and is, the great fathomless dark that existed before anything else and which still exists today, surrounding and permeating the realms of existence.

'The Great Essence is like a huge, unimaginable black womb, like a dream waiting to take form. And suddenly way back who-knows-when, a spark came out of that void. The spark was an idea, an energy, and from that we believe, the most ancient ones were formed – ideas, primal ideas, and energies given form.'

'And the Great Essence is what then? A god?'

Agnes chuckled softly. 'No, we don't believe so. Thornish people don't believe in things like gods. Not in the way most people think of such things anyway. We think of the Great Essence as the beginning of everything we know and while we do believe it is intelligent in its way it is simply primordially ancient beyond our ability to conceive. It's like the ancient glacial ice that is so far down it is pitch black…and from that all the streams flow. Some Thornish people liken the Great Essence to what our Native friends call the Great Mystery, and by Great Mystery we mean precisely that. It's mysterious.'

I suggested that the Dark Mother might be like a river that flowed from that great dark glacier she spoke of and she patted my hand softly in response.

'Something like that,' she said. 'We see the Old Ones something like that. It is said that there are many Old Ones, some very ancient who were the first ones to come from the gateway the Dark Mother guards. Some of these are aware of us, some are not. Some don't care. We are simply too insignificant to matter to them. Can you imagine that? Something so vast and old, something so far beyond us we are like germs on a rock compared to a woman driving by in a car? Some know we are here and don't like us very much either. They can be dangerous. However, we do have some that take an interest in us and those are the ones we generally refer to as the Elder Kin.'

'The Dark Mother is one of the Elder Kin then?'

'She is more like the grandmother of them, but like them we believe she is aware of us and generally well disposed towards our kind. Not to ever be treated with disrespect because then she can be quite the opposite of caring. She is the essence of balance.'

Agnes was quiet for some time and we simply sat there in her living room, lit only by the glow of the two small candles and what light flowed in from the dining room. Before us the enigmatic figure of the Dark Lady, the keeper of the keys, also stood silently, as if pondering us from her rustic shrine.

'There is a lot I want to show you and teach you, now that we have come to an agreement,' Agnes said at last. 'What I ask in return for what I'll teach you is this and only this: When you find someone worthy pass on what you know and above that, cherish the sacred balance in all things.'

'I will do that,' I replied.

Agnes sipped from her coffee cup. 'That's good to know because tomorrow I am going to show you how you can get much closer to this sacred Lady…and indeed much closer to the Black Root.'

* * *

The next morning Agnes and I went for a nice walk along the river that flowed not that far from her house. We ate only a light breakfast and I after we had walked for a couple of hours my stomach started to complain.

As we walked Agnes said she wanted to show me a ritual that had come into the Thornish way from Europe long ago. One of the traditions which had influenced the Black Talon Society as it was today came from an enigmatic fellow named Agnarr who moved to Canada from Norway in the 1950s. Agnarr had been a medical doctor and an amateur historian of sorts as well as a member of a Germanic secret society that focused on the revival of ancient pagan ways. His teacher had been a sorcerer of sorts who himself had come from an even more cryptic order. The traditions of Agnarr and his teacher, Augustus, made a considerable impact on Ari and his brothers back in the day, and as the Raven Lodge broke new ground for the Black Talon Society some of these old ways found their way into the Thornish traditions.

One of these traditions which had been adopted was known as the Halls of Silence. It involved setting aside a sanctified space in a specific setting so that the barriers between the seeker and the primal forces might be made a little easier to penetrate.

Agnes told me that in her opinion one of the best things that someone new to the traditions of the Thornwood could do was to go and sit in the Halls of Silence. The more sense a person has for the realities around them, the unseen worlds that surround and permeate everything we know, the better they might be able to understand what it was that people like the Shar had set out to do.

'This first time I will sit with you,' Agnes said. 'I think it will be a good thing for us to share this experience. The ritual is conducted in silence, though,' she added.

After we returned to the house Agnes wasted no time in getting to work. She left me for a short time, asking me to go and change into something loose and comfortable. I settled on a sweatshirt and some loose jogging pants and was waiting for her in the kitchen when she came back for me. In moments, with a slight grin on her face, she asked me to come with her, leading me down to the little wine cellar room. She took only a moment to grab a small blanket and a pillow from the couch before she led the way.

When we arrived, she offered me a light hooded robe from a peg in the wall. 'As with the Hollowing, it's good to have something in which you can close off the outer world and focus on your senses.'

I took the robe and put it on. It opened in the front, had wide sleeves and a deep hood. The material felt like a very soft linen and was light brown in color.

'Formalities,' Agnes said suddenly, as though she had remembered it at the last moment. 'In our tradition, when we decide we are going to teach someone, we become Wataan to them. Yes, here we go with another strange word. *Wataan* is a distinctly Thornish word but it originally comes from a Germanic word meaning someone who has done things before, someone who has waded through hardship and learned a few things. Anyway, you and I will seldom use the term but I thought you should know it.'

'It's kind of like the Japanese word Sensei then?'

'A bit like that, I guess,' she replied. 'But for the most part I am happy enough with just plain old Agnes.'

'By the way,' she added, 'while this ritual is a very powerful one and I do it myself a fair bit, it's not a requirement in your training. I just thought it might be something you would appreciate.'

'It's not a Thornish custom, then?'

'Oh, it is,' she replied. 'It was one of those things that came in when the Raven Lodge was established, but it's not a necessary part of the Learner's journey. In my experience, while any Thornish person can do this ritual, I feel it has a little more to offer to women. Maybe I am wrong about that.'

In a relatively short time I had learned a lot from Agnes about the tradition she followed. After I completed the Hollowing ritual she took me aside and explained more about the Thornish way. The lion's share of these teachings took place in two environments: outdoors, whether that was on her property or out in the local wild places, or in her cozy and magical living room.

Not long after my first Hollowing she sat me down in the living room with the requisite pot of steaming tea and tray of delicious baked treats. She told me she thought she had been somewhat remiss in not explaining the really bare bones of the Thornish way and she figured she should lay it all on the table for me. She said since I had decided to walk in this way I was showing tremendous confidence in her and she was teaching me a good way.

'To earn the right of being called Wataan, or even *Wataana* if you are female, in this tradition it's important to teach clearly and well,' she told me. 'There is little room for what the graylings call faith in our traditions. We prefer confidence and evidence over faith, so it's important to get the lessons across very clearly.'

Agnes explained that the current incarnation of the Black Talon in the Middle World (what the Thornish folk generally call this planet Earth in this time and space) is generally known as the Thornish Nation. This term comes from two sources. The first one is a tale called *Raven Visits the Thornwood*. This tale was in existence long before the founders of the Raven Lodge were initiated and tells of an experience Raven had with the Ladies of Wyrd. The second source for the term Thornish comes from a powerful Vision experienced by two of the founders of the Raven Lodge; a Vision of a man seeking enlightenment in a dark wood of Thorn trees. Agnes explained that in both cases the thorn trees are seen as sacred teachers of the hard-way of mystical teachings, a way of ordeal and primal experiential learning.

'The way of the Thornwood was never meant to be a soft-way, a mere book learning or musing way,' Agnes added. 'Unless you invest yourself and really make offerings of yourself, the Elder Ones will not see any reason to give you anything in return. That's why we get out there and sometimes experience hardship and even suffering in order to learn what we need to learn.'

After Agnes told me about the origins of the term Thornish she went on to fill me in on the structure of things. 'If a person hears of our ways and wants to learn more they probably can do that,' she said. 'Maybe one day one of us will write a book or something. Who knows? If you want to live in a Thornish way we figure that it is a good thing, good for the Earth and the sacred balance. However, if one wants to be Shar then one has to go through an initiatory process.'

'And the Black Talon Society?' I asked, trying to fit things together in my mind.

'To earn the bloodmark you have to go through the process of initiations,' she replied. 'To be a member of the Black Talon Society and to have the right to refer to oneself as 'Shar' a person will have to be initiated.'

'How does initiation work?'

Agnes gave me that mysterious look I had seen on her before. It was a kind of reserved, analyzing look that said *I am trying to decide whether I should answer this or not.*

After a moment she said, 'Only a Shar can forge a Shar. What that means is unless you are an initiated Master in the tradition you cannot ever bring anyone else into our inner ways. A Hollowing and acceptance by an initiated teacher makes one a Learner.. To go beyond that you must be taught directly and in person and you need to be given a proper ordeal and crossing to be one of us.'

'A crossing?'

'Another word for initiation. Something that you yourself are working towards.'

'So no postal correspondence courses or telephone calls, eh?' I smiled.

Agnes shook her head, smiling.

'No,' she said. 'Those things are a great way to meet people but in our way they are not a good way to teach people. We feel it is also disrespectful to our elders and our ancestors and to our tribal traditions. We consider our ways to be the tribal property of our folk and to give it all out too freely would not be the right thing to do. Also, it could be dangerous to give out certain types of knowledge to the uninitiated.'

'I see,' I replied somewhat hesitantly.

Agnes' face went from an amused look to a very serious expression all in an instant. For a second I was reminded that she was indeed a Master teacher and held the keys to some pretty powerful traditions in her hands.

'I think you begin to see, Carolyn, my student,' she said softly. 'But beginning to see is a start.'

We sat in silence for a moment before Agnes said, 'We are very serious about this, my Raven-friend. Dead serious. This is not some fantasy game we play here but the carrying on of a very real and sometimes very potent tradition. It is not for the common folk and certainly not for graylings. We have ways of knowing who has been taught in a proper, traditional way and who has not been. The results of someone falsely claiming to be one of us, one of the initiated inner circle…well, let's just say that there would likely be very unpleasant consequences which would fall on that person.'

'We are what some have called 'forest mages.'' she said. 'But in reality we are simply implements of the sacred balance. Yes, there are deep spiritual acts and even what outsiders might call magical workings in the tradition, but the greater picture is that we learn and grow so we can serve our world in this existence. For instance, I am what is called a Farer. A Farer is a person who goes on many spiritual journeys by various means in order to gain power and knowledge.'

'Like a Medicine Man?'

'Somewhat like that, yes,' she said. 'But we try not to use Native terms or walk in their ways. We revere them as great teachers but we respect that their ways are not our ways.'

Once a person is chosen to learn the deeper traditions, Agnes continued, they are called a Learner. A Learner is the lowest level of student and spends considerable time being taught things about the tradition. If a Learner decides the tradition is not for them they can simply and politely walk away. Beyond that, once a person swears oaths and makes certain spiritual pacts walking away is not so easy. That was why there were levels of learning and responsibility.

'Pretty fancy name for it, eh?' Agnes chuckled. 'Learner says it all. The job of the Learner is to learn all they can because they are working their way to their first Deepening. The Learner is proving to us – and to themselves – that they are worthy of being considered for full membership in the tribe and they are being considered as worthy to perform a Deepening. In some ways, you are already past the level of understanding that many might have of us, Carolyn. You are fortunate enough to have teachers who are members of the Black Talon Society.'

I knew this and I once again told Agnes how glad I was I had found my way to her and her friends.

'As I said before, a person who learns of our ways might consider themselves Thornish, but without initiation they will always be Learners. Initiation must come from an initiated member of the Society. The deeper ways are not something that can be taught through a book or by any sort of correspondence. In your situation there is a good chance you will be initiated eventually and allowed to go on a Deepening.'

A Deepening is a ritual quest that all Thornish people must go on in order to become initiates. I was told it is very vaguely similar to the Native Vision Quest but also contains other components which are uniquely Thornish.

There are three Greater Deepenings that every Shar is expected to take in their lives as they grow further in the tradition. There are also Lesser Deepenings which are designed to enrich and enhance various aspects of a Thornish person's life. The Greater Deepenings are almost like ordeals or tests that a person takes in order to be worthy of the initiatory level before them. Agnes explained that each of the Greater Deepenings is more demanding than the one which came before it and in each Deepening there is a certain level of risk and danger to the person performing it.

'The first Deepening is what makes a student something greater. It means you are really past the point of being someone who is simply content to walk as a Thornish person,' Agnes told me. 'It is usually three days and three nights in duration. When a person completes the first Deepening they are eligible to be given the initiation ceremony. Once they have done that they become known as Seekers. Seekers are the true apprentices of the tradition and they are in the inner circle of learning.'

'Seekers are the ones who have access to the inner knowledge then?'

'Yes,' she replied. 'During one's time as a Seeker one can learn many things and usually this is the time period where people get a feel for the tribal specialties they may want to look into. Some are dancers, some are crafters, some become really proficient hunters or root-workers, healers and such. Others become Farers like I am. Following this period of apprenticeship, a person is prepared for the second of the Greater Deepenings. This is the Master's Deepening and it is usually six days and nights in duration.'

The Masters make up the core of the tradition and are the teachers and keepers of the Thornish Lore. Masters are considered to be the backbone of the Black Talon Society and are held in great respect.

'Beyond this, years down the road, a person may decide they want to walk the road of the last of the Greater Deepenings,' Agnes explained. 'This is the Elder's Deepening. It is a sojourn of nine days and nights in the wilderness and is held in high regard by everyone. A Shar Elder is a very respectable person in our ways and someone who has completed the Elder's Deepening is considered to be pretty wise indeed.'

'Are there any Shar Elders around here?' I asked.

'There are not many at this point.' Agnes replied. 'Not everyone performs the Elder's Deepening and there have been quite a few old Masters who were satisfied simply with being Masters. Quite a few of those who do become Elders, or those worthy to be called that, have a tendency to simply fade out. By that I mean they become more and more mystical and tend to eventually disappear from the world as we know it. However, there is one I can think of who you will get a chance to meet one of these days soon, I hope.'

I was suddenly filled with nervous tension thinking about such a meeting. What would such a person be like?

My thoughts began to drop away and I realized Agnes was waving her hand in front of me, trying to get me to break free of my reverie. 'Earth to Carolyn. You there, Carolyn?' She grinned.

'Sorry, I was thinking. There is just so much to think about.'

'I understand,' she said. 'I was talking about formalities and the role of the Wataan and then you got this fuzzy look on your face and tuned out a bit.'

'Sorry about that,' I said. 'No intention to be rude.'

'No offense taken. I was like that quite a bit when this was new to me as well.'

Agnes walked over to the door on the far side of the room. I had wondered about it the very first time I sat in that room but had not asked about it. Now she opened it and beckoned me to come have a look.

On the other side of the door was an amazing little room. It was not large but it more than made up for that with the way it had been constructed. It was maybe twenty feet long by ten feet across, about the size of a storage room, and perhaps that is what it was originally built to be. But Agnes had gotten a hold of it and done something wonderful.

The walls and ceiling of the little room were plastered over in a rich, reddish brown plaster creating a cavern-like look. The walls had little niches and alcoves built into them so it looked as though they had been carved into the walls of a rock cave. At the end of the room the wall was similarly formed and had a pedestal on which sat a smaller version of the Dark Mother statue I had seen in Agnes' living room. There were maybe nine or ten niches in each wall. Some of these had little glowing candles in glass holders in them and others had small statues of various god and goddess forms in them. Most of the forms were very primal, almost Paleolithic in nature and the light from the candles, all red and orange, gave the place a very magical, otherworldly feel. The room was not cool or damp as one might expect such a subterranean room to be.

The floor was made of polished wood and though it appeared to be quite old looked very solid and well kept. On the floor was a large meditation-style cushion and a small woolen blanket much like the ones Agnes had carried in.

She ushered me into the small room and motioned me to sit down. 'This room is well ventilated so you don't have to worry,' she said. 'It's the chamber I use to meditate when I want to feel closer to the Old Ones. It's my own little version of the Halls of Silence. I hope you can find something of value as you sit here.'

'It's beautiful,' I said.

Agnes smiled. 'When I come here I go silent and ask the Elder Ones for their guidance. You might be surprised at what comes to you. Stay as long or as little as you like. I will be waiting in the other room when you are done.'

In a moment more, Agnes was gone, closing the door softly and leaving me alone in that cozy and magical little room. I sat down cross-legged on the large comfortable pillow and arranged myself looking straight at the back of the room, towards the statue of the Dark Mother. I saw no need for the hood on the robe at that time so I left down.

I let myself relax and tried to absorb the atmosphere of the room. I noticed the subtle scent of herbs in the room and suspected that while I was off in my room changing Agnes had come down here and burned incense as she lit all the candles for me.

The room seemed to become somewhat dimmer as I sat there on the cushion, practicing my breathing as I had been taught. I thought that as my eyes adjusted the room would seem brighter, yet this did not happen. Perhaps it had something to do with the energy in the room…or perhaps it was just my imagination. No matter. It was very relaxing and I had no trouble calming myself and simply breathing.

Without realizing it my hand found the dark Lore-Stone hanging on its thong around my neck. Agnes told me that part of the reason it is called a Lore-Stone is because in Thornish belief stone has a great memory and readily absorbs energy in many forms. When a person with a Lore Stone has experiences, a part of that experience is taken into the stone. This, I was told, could help a person later when they need a powerful talisman. When a Thornish person passed on their Lore Stone would be hung from the hearth of their Hall or Lodge. That way their good energy and experience would not entirely be taken from this world when their body died.

For a long while I simply held on to the feeling of being there in that soft, potent place, holding my Lore Stone in my hand. After awhile I began to feel like I was somehow being absorbed into the atmosphere of the room. I felt as though I was somehow sinking into the floor and softly becoming part of the room. A great, warm calm filled me as I sat there and I felt more at home than I had even in the welcoming rooms of Agnes' house. There was something very special in that place and I wondered if it might have something to do with the many goddess-style figures or perhaps the energy that had been generated there by Agnes as she meditated.

The room was very, very quiet. I could hear the slight sounds the little candles made as they burned in their glass holders and I could hear my own heartbeat quite well.

And noticing these things, then setting them aside gently as I had been taught to do, I went back into a soft, gentle state of mind and simply allowed myself to be. I didn't ask the Elder Ones for anything. I just sat there in the silent glow of that little room absorbing as much of the experience as I could.

I am not sure when the whispering sounds started. I am only sure that when I became aware of them in my meditation they did not slip away. They stayed and as I became more conscious of them they became more obvious.

I placed one hand to my ear to block out the sound, to see if it was coming from inside the room. It seemed, however, that the sound was actually coming from somewhere inside of my head, inside of me.

I was not frightened by this. Rather I was fascinated by it. It sounded something like women whispering together in a hallway or perhaps an alleyway. It was one of those times when you think you can almost understand the words, but not quite, and it was as frustrating as it was fascinating. I tried to focus myself into a deeper state so I might hear what was being said, but this did not do me much good.

So I simply stopped trying and let the strange, whispering sound slide off into the background. I never lost track of it but I was no longer paying strict attention to it either.

This went on for a considerable time before the hairs on the back of my neck went up and I felt an electrical charge of cold energy flow down my spine. At first I thought Agnes had come in through the door to get me, but a moment later I realized that was not the case. Agnes had not come into the room, but something had…and it had not come in through the door.

The presence came in suddenly and felt like it was directly behind me, though as I turned to look I could see nothing there. The presence felt very real and yet it didn't feel menacing or bad. It started to feel more familiar the longer it stayed. I decided this must be another aspect of the energy of the small room and so I forced myself to remain calm and tried to go back to meditating.

It took awhile but eventually I managed to put the feeling of the presence into the background just as I had the sound of the whispering voices. If there was something that these things had come to do or to teach I figured they would do so in their own good time. Back I went to my breathing: Count from one to nine, breathe in, breathe out and at nine begin again.

In my mind's eye I was drifting through a dimly lit forest. It smelled acrid, the way woods smell when there are lots of autumn leaves all over the place and the fall is well underway. The feel of the place was damp and slightly chilly though it was not uncomfortable.

In the dream or vision I seemed to be following a trail through the darkening trees. Finally, I came out in a small grassy clearing and in the middle of that clearing, dominating it, was a large mossy, grass-covered mound. In front of me was a stone-framed opening and beyond that there was a dark rectangle opening that penetrated the mound.

I felt afraid and tried to stop myself from moving towards the opening. I slowed down but could not stop. I did not want to go up to that doorway and I certainly did not want to go into the burial mound. No matter what Agnes had told me about the sacred beauty of such things there was a very powerful fear in me about the mound and I did not want to see what would happen if I went inside.

I was thinking about shaking myself out of my meditative state when my movement suddenly stopped. The whispering voices had also stopped. I was only about a foot or so from the threshold of the deep black door and I had not been forced inside after all.

And then, as my eyes adjusted, I realized with a shock that in front of me was not just an impenetrable black place leading deep within the mound. Instead I looked out into intergalactic space with billions of bright stars shining in sparkling clusters. There was even the foggy spiral of some galaxy off in the blue-black distance.

I was amazed. My heart was beating faster as I stared into this impossible-seeming vista. It was like there was an entire universe living inside of that big grim-looking hill.

The voices came back and this time they were coming from somewhere to my left. I turned and saw three shrouded figures standing off to one side, not far from where the forest ended. They did not approach me but instead stood there watching and whispering. I still couldn't hear what they were saying. Maybe I was never meant to.

From the same trail, I had walked came another figure. This one, like the others, was clad in a dark cloak and her face was shrouded so I could not see her features underneath her hood. This one held a long staff with a sharp blade on the top in one hand. As the figure drew closer I could see the top of the staff glinting brightly in the light of the dying sun. It looked like a sickle of some sort, crescent-moon-shaped and glowing gold in the cold light.

The shrouded one approached me and I was able to turn completely and look at her. I had no fear now. It was nothing like when I thought I was going to get pushed into the barrow mound. Instead there was a feeling of familiarity and almost…kindness coming from the figure. I could not put my finger on it but somehow I knew this person.

'As you know me, daughter, you know I will not cause you harm. I am breath to your breath, kin to your kin and blood to your blood,' came the voice that sounded more like wind creeping through a window on a winter's day than the kind of sound a human could ever make. Like the whispering women's voices it was coming from inside of my head rather than through my ears. It was a very strange and unsettling feeling.

The figure came to a stop only a few feet from where I stood by the threshold to that impossibly beautiful starry world. She radiated energy that felt not wintery, like her voice did, but rather like the sun on a warm spring day. I realized with a start that I could now see the slightest form of her face beneath the cowl and my mind spun in confusion. Her face looked something like a moon-white skull and at the same time was a very elegant- looking woman's face. The two images shared the same space without one or the other settling into a solid form. Her long hair flowed around her face and it was either gray or white. I began thinking that if I tried to look at her any more I would probably develop a headache. It was as though her form was something that human eyes were never meant to look on or comprehend. She was beautiful in an unearthly way that even now I cannot properly describe.

'You are the Dark Mother,' I managed to say.

The figure nodded and suddenly I felt a joy I had seldom felt before. I had to restrain myself from suddenly throwing my arms around her in a loving daughterly embrace and I had no idea why.

'I am the mother of all mothers, yes, child,' she said softly, and this time the voice went from being like a whispering wind to a sound like that of birds in flight over water. 'And when you come to me I know that you will come with grace and courage. This is why you are here, daughter of Raven. This is why you are here. To learn to teach, to fly, and then to come home.'

'Are you really a goddess of death?' I asked, shuddering and longing to hug this great-grandmother of all great-grandmothers at the same time.

'I am the gate keeper. I am the beginning of the wheel and the end of the road…and the sign that points to many other places and many other roads.'

'I think you are my grandmother.' It was all I could think of to say.

And the dark, shrouded figure nodded once again and I felt like the deepest sorrow and the most profound joy had come flooding out from her and into my own heart. I could barely contain myself. I knew that tears were flooding down my cheeks as I knelt in the small room, just as they splashed down my face as I stood in that sunset-glowing otherworld. This figure before me that looked so menacing, with a face like a skull and a beautiful patrician woman's all at that same time, was to me like a bubbling spring of the deepest human emotions. I also had a feeling of timeless and powerful yet stern love there. It was the kind of love that could either be very kind and forgiving or quite the opposite if the circumstances demanded it. Being in her presence was nearly overpowering and yet I knew it was also a feeling a person could find themselves addicted if they stayed too long in that place.

'Walk in a good way, daughter,' the voice-like-birds said softly. 'Learn and grow and serve the balance.'

And then the figure, my great-great-great-great-grandmother who I found I had so much love for, turned and glided back the way she had come, into the dark blackness of the woods. The three whispering figures were also gone and I realized I had begun fading back into the world I shared with Agnes. I wanted to hold on for a while and stay there in that mysterious place but I found that I was weak from the emotions that had been flowing through me. Finally I let go and returned to the place of the glowing candles and the little cave-like room.

I was overwhelmed with what had just happened and I wondered how I had existed for so long without realizing that there was so much…more out there, just beyond our ability to see. My face was indeed wet with tears, as was my shirt and the front of the robe. My back and neck ached, though my legs, surprisingly, did not.

After a time, after I collected myself and wiped the wetness from my face, I got shakily to my feet and stood for a moment in the deep and special silence of that sacred little place. I bowed slightly to the figure of the Dark Mother there on her little pedestal and I silently gave thanks to any other spirits there in the room. I felt so humbled and lucky and special to have experienced the things that I had. In the past I thought that the really cool adventures always happened to somebody else but never to me.

I was wrong about that. Very wrong, it turned out.

Eventually I forced myself to turn around and go to the door. When I opened it I saw Agnes had finished her own meditations and was now sitting at the small table. It only took a moment for her to realize, seeing my face and reading my body language, that something powerful had happened to me in there. She came over to me and we shared a tearful hug.

'I met her in there,' I said.

I did not have to elaborate as Agnes knew exactly who I was talking about. 'I kind of thought you might,' she said.

'You honor many Elder Kin and spirits but I can tell that the Dark Lady has a special place in your heart,' I said once the trembling in my voice faded away.

'Over the years she has become very special to me,' Agnes replied. 'She has become my Hearth-Mistress or Matron, so to speak. She has been a powerful force for change and healing within me.'

I could see there was a very powerful connection between Agnes and the Dark Mother.

Agnes rolled up her sleeve and for the very first time I realized she had several tattoos on her left forearm. One of them, amazingly enough, I recognized immediately and my mind scrambled to try and place where I had seen it before. It looked vaguely like two eyes standing opposite to one another, as if one of them was looking down at itself, reflected in still water.

At last I remembered. I had seen the exact same design tattooed on another arm in exactly the same spot…on Russell's skin.

But this was not the tattoo Agnes indicated when she rolled her sleeve further up to expose her bicep. There on her skin was an all black design showing the head and shoulders of a cloaked figure superimposed on a large spiral. I could barely make out the face of the figure and she looked vaguely skeletal, much like the mysterious Lady who had come to me in the Halls of Silence. It was a beautiful piece rendered by a very talented artist.

'This is a blood-mark,' Agnes said. 'I don't go around showing it off to just anybody so you must be special or something.' With that she smiled and rolled her sleeve down.

'It's my dedication to her, actually,' she added. 'It's a continual offering that tells her I am her student and granddaughter. It also reminds me, day to day, of my commitment to the old ways and to her.'

I was impressed. A tattoo like that was a permanent mark, not easy to remove.

'And the other one, the one that looks like the Native style eyes?'

'That's the oldest one I have,' she replied. 'It's the mark of the Black Talon Society. You might earn one like that yourself if you play your cards right.'

I knew I had a considerable road to travel to be worthy of something like that. I was further impressed that these folks had permanent tribal marks put on their skin.

'And the other one, the one that looks like two knives?'

'That would be a Master's sigil,' she said. 'When you become a Shar Master you will have the right to that one. It's a steeper path to such things like that, as I am sure you can imagine.'

I thought I knew a fair amount about these mysterious people and their equally mysterious tradition, yet in the end I actually knew very little. My gut had been telling me all along, however, that this was right for me and that somehow I was in the process of coming home.

'I will learn everything you have to teach me,' was all I said to that one.

Agnes patted me on the shoulder and gathered up her blanket and pillow.

'We always wait for the candles to burn down,' she said and pulled a large thermos and two cups from her bag. 'So let's stay awhile down here and talk a bit while the Elder Ones are appeased.'

7. Raven

When autumn came I had been living at Agnes' house for well over two months. Agnes taught me many things, not only about her traditions but also the ways of farm life. I began to feel like I was taking advantage of her generosity, even though I contributed to things like groceries and supplies. I still felt like I wasn't doing enough.

I finally told Agnes about this and she simply smiled.

'Your head is still trapped in the Lie, little sister,' she said. 'Part of being awake—really awake—is realizing you don't have to go along with all of the old bullshit that mainstream culture lays on us. You are my guest and, more than that, you are a friend who is staying with me. Also, you are my student. Bug me about paying rent or any other such nonsense again and I will smack you with a broom,' she said, and we both had a little chuckle.

Agnes spoke about at length about the need for more people to wake up, to snap out of the illusion of centuries of mainstream programming, and realize that the world was a much larger place.

'If anything, life is stranger than ever. People have been convinced to give up their land and even their extended families to go work as drones in the city. How old, for instance, is the United States? Two hundred years this past summer. Do you think they are much better off after all that time? I think they have gotten worse,' she said. 'We are not much better up here. The world becomes more decadent every day and more damage is being done. This needs to stop and there are only two ways that will happen. Either we will become extinct or we will wake up. I prefer the latter.'

Agnes liked to do things the 'old way.' She said the Thornish way was not about trying to live in the past, it was about trying to live a good and balanced life in the present using wisdom gained from the past.

'Authority is an illusion,' she told me. 'The only authority that has ever existed is the laws of the multiverse, and from that the laws of nature. There is an old saying that goes, 'the greatest scam the devil ever pulled was convincing people that he didn't exist.' Well, as usual, the Christians stole that one off of someone else, but it makes a point. For a very long time people have been brainwashed into believing that anyone can tell them what to do. We all walk our own path, sister.'

I listened to her and nodded my head. Russell had said something similar and it really made a lot of sense to me. Since meeting Russell, and coming to Pemberton, I realized I was doing much more than learning warrior skills. I was re-learning how to perceive reality.

'I'll say one last time that you do more than your share around here. Let's leave it at that,' Agnes said with a grin.

And so I went about my work helping Agnes on her small farm, sitting with her, and learning all I could absorb about the tradition she followed. The Thornish way is, at its core, a path that follows the ancient animistic beliefs. It evolved out of a blending of the ways of the Northern Europeans who had come to this land and the ways of the Native people who had first formed the Black Talon Society.

The two cultures that now came together in the secret society were always respectful of one another but over the years, Agnes explained, there had been difficulty in keeping the two sets of core traditions separate. Some said that there was too much Indian influence and others worried that the Germanic ways might fade away altogether, yet they always found a way to keep the balance. In more recent times, when the Society no longer needed to remain so secretive and Indian people were not actively prosecuted for practicing their traditional ways, there had again been talk about the mixed culture of the society.

Back in the late 1950s a movement had begun within the Society which saw the old lodges wanting to fade away and disappear into the wild places, where the initiates could continue in a more Native style fashion, more like the wild mountain men that had originally founded the Society.

Some did not agree with this thinking. They wanted to go out into the world and teach others about the mysteries they had discovered. They wanted to help bring balance back to the world in a much larger way. In the end there were younger members who asked that they be allowed to form their own lodge. With this lodge they would then go out into the world more openly to teach.

The elders of the old lodge agreed to this, seeing it as a way of balance, and they gave the new lodge their blessing.

'What we have here in the modern day is the result of that new lodge being formed,' Agnes told me. 'The new lodge is quite different from the old lodge and this is the way it was intended to be. The elders of the old ways knew that in order to move forward the tradition would need to adapt and change with the modern world. Most of the old timers didn't want to do that and were content to go off into the wild lands. However, they wanted some of their ways to continue and knew that the best way for that to happen was to let the new lodge be formed.'

'It seems rather confusing to me that they did that,' I said. 'I mean, they had this thing going for a long time and then they kind of split into two groups.'

'There was simply less reason to stay hidden, I think,' Agnes replied. 'Don't get me wrong, in the late 50s there was still persecution of pagans and Indians and the need to stay underground was still very real, but there were those who thought it was less than before. Some of them were used to being hidden and rather liked the isolation. Others wanted to do something a little different and out of respect this was allowed. It happened very slowly, I was told. Very quietly. Even the people in the new lodge were very cautious. It wasn't till the mid to late '60s that the new lodge made any real move to reveal their existence.'

'So the elders knew this change was coming and they didn't get in its way.'

'Pretty much, yes.'

I nodded. It was all still terribly new to me, this way of thinking and being, and the fact that I was training to become part of something so much deeper than I had ever imagined was quite overwhelming to think about.

Once, when we were sitting out on a green patch of grass down by the creek having our lunch, I asked Agnes how many Thornish people there actually were.

'Hmm...' she said by way of a reply and for a few minutes afterward said nothing more. Finally she told me she didn't really have an answer and she seriously doubted anyone these days could give a truly accurate answer.

'You see, the term Thornish has only been around since about 1958 when the Raven Lodge came into being. Before that, members were simply brothers of the Black Talon Society and of whatever Lodge they belonged to. The Raven Lodge was founded by seven men and each of them brought their own power into it. Of the seven, only five of them were Black Talon. The others were initiated during the founding of the Raven Lodge. So if you count those guys as being the first then my guess would be less than twenty altogether.'

'And the Black Talon Society?'

'Who knows?' she replied. 'Some people think it is hundreds of years old and others think its much more recent. There are said to be lodges back east in Ontario and Manitoba and Alberta. It's hard to say how many there ever were.'

Agnes pulled a big pickle out of a jar and bit into it. 'The Black Talon Society is very exclusive,' she said after a moment longer. 'A person does not ask to join but rather, if they are worthy, they may be offered the honor of joining. This is the same with any of the lodges which were a part of it or formed from it.'

Agnes took another bite of her pickle and chewed it thoughtfully for a minute more. I could tell she was thinking very carefully about what she was going to say before she said it.

'And an initiate is a member of the lodges,' I said.

'Yes,' Agnes replied. 'The word *Shar* is a term to describe a person who is Thornish and who has been initiated into one of the lodges. Hey, the way we walk is a good, healthy balanced way. To be Thornish and yet not a part of the lodges is still a great achievement.'

Agnes finished her pickle and wiped her mouth in satisfaction. 'But you know, I am not as much of an authority on such things as others are,' she said. 'And later today I am taking you up to meet my teacher so maybe you can ask him.'

It suddenly struck me that I had not heard a great amount about who her teacher actually was. She had spoken much about a man called Raven, who had been the original founder of the Raven Lodge. This was THE guy who took the old way of the Society and with the blessing of the elders formed a very new kind of warrior's lodge. I realized that if it were not for this fellow I would probably not even be here in the valley learning what I was learning.

And I knew very little about this person other than what I had already been told. What kind of person was he? Was he some venerable old senior citizen in a wheelchair now, or was he something else altogether? I told Agnes I was looking forward to meeting Raven but I was also a bit nervous. After all, I was about to shake hands with someone who, for all intents and purposes, was not only a legend in the Society but also a great warrior and a powerful mage.

Agnes heard me out and then laughed. 'Well, since you have already met him and didn't get turned into a frog I see no reason for you to be nervous this time.'

'What?' I asked, thrown off completely.

'Yeah, you already met him,' Agnes said. 'Russ told me you guys ran into him in town that time.'

My mind spun for a second as I searched my memory. Finally I realized that there was only one person who fit the bill.

'You mean Ari, that friend of Russell's? He's Raven?'

Agnes looked at me with a Cheshire cat kind of look on her face.

'Who else did you expect him to be?'

* * *

Ari seemed quite happy to see us later that afternoon and ushered us into his beautiful little home in the woods. It was quite an old house but looked as though it had seen a lot of care and attention over the years. As we passed through the living room I noticed the unusually large stone hearth with an equally large black-scabbarded longsword on the mantel.

Like the master of the house, who gave off a very mysterious and powerful vibe, his dwelling also gave off a very enigmatic yet comforting vibration. It felt like a great many acts of power had been performed in this home.

Ari led us into the kitchen where we sat at a large, well-polished pine table for coffee and muffins. At first we chatted about local things. Ari asked how I was getting along at Agnes' place and I told him a little about my adventures without going into too much detail.

After a time Agnes looked at her watch, finished her cup of coffee, and bade us both a farewell. 'I'll be back around dinner time to get you,

Carolyn,' she said. 'Ari should be finished with you by then.'

Ari chuckled. 'Or rather, she might be done with me by then.'

And with that Agnes left, this time through the screen door on the other side of Ari's large bright kitchen.

After a few minutes Ari ushered me out into the back yard. Not far away from the back porch there was a well-built fire-pit complete with a crackling fire already lit. We went over and sat down opposite each other on a couple of cut logs.

'So,' Ari said, 'Agnes tells me that you are ready to learn more. If that is the case I can tell you a few things.'

At that I had to chuckle. 'From what Agnes says you are the guy who knows everything there ever was to know about the tradition, being the founder and all.'

And then it was Ari's turn to laugh. It was a loud, joyful sound which erupted so unexpectedly it caught me off guard.

When Ari finished laughing and slapping his knee in merriment he looked at me, still grinning. 'Hardly, my dear. I may have been one of the founders of the lodge here but I was just one man. Additionally, I am part of something that goes back a long way which holds many secrets that not even I have completely unlocked yet.'

'But still…you are Raven. *The* Raven that Agnes has mentioned quite a bit.'

'Yes, I am Raven. That is the name which was given to me about a hundred years ago.' He chuckled again. 'Sometimes it seems a very long time ago that I was a young fella so full of piss and vinegar…probably too much for my own good.'

From beside his log seat Ari took an object wrapped in a piece of deer skin. 'But on to business,' he said, now looking at me in a far more serious way. 'We have only met the one time before and even though you know about me from others and probably figure I can be trusted, there is a custom in our way that should be observed. When a female student is brought before a male teacher we give her a gift that will prove the sincerity of the Master and create an atmosphere of peace between them.' Ari stood up and offered me the deerskin bundle.

I accepted it and was rather surprised at its considerable weight. There inside the orange-brown softness of the skin was an absolutely gorgeous, wickedly sharp-looking knife. It was about eight inches long with a handle made from a piece of antler split in half. The handle was pinned to the metal of the blade with two bright brass rivets. The blade was a shiny black metal that was slightly curved, like a claw. The edge, which gleamed like a razor, ran up the inside of the 'claw,' leaving the other edge, the back edge apparently, unsharpened.

'I don't know what to say.'

'We call it a Frith-knife,' he said quietly. 'It is very sharp, so be careful with it. I will see what I can do about getting you a sheath to go along with it.'

'Its for me?'

'Yes. It's a thing that was once only given to women in our tradition. Actually, it was Agnes who wanted the custom changed to include men as well. She thought that it would be more reflective of balance that way. The Frith-Knife is a peace-maker and it tells anyone who receives it that they are, and always will be, empowered here in our sacred circles.'

'Empowered?' I asked.

'Women are deeply respected in our tradition,' he said. And Ari related to me a story from the tradition that went like this:

Long ago, among the tribes of northern Europe, there were two bands whose chiefs desired an alliance. One of the ways this was accomplished was through marriage and so various offerings of brides or grooms were made between the chiefs. However, in this situation, the leader of one tribe was not male but a beautiful and powerful woman. The chief of the other tribe was a powerful man who had never married. He was entranced by the beautiful woman chieftain and made an offer of betrothal to her that included much treasure and many horses. While the woman chief found her counterpart to be very attractive she had to think of the image this might present to her people. She also feared losing her authority if she were to marry this man and so she told him that she would not marry him unless he could prove to her that he was a man of honor and would not try to steal her leadership over her people.

The man thought about this dilemma long and hard and in the end offered to swear a mighty oath before the people that he would share leadership of the combined tribe. The woman chieftain agreed to this and the man did as he said he would. The oath was sworn and the two bands became as one tribe.

On the evening of their wedding the man took one step further. In the candlelight of their tent he offered his bride a gleaming, wickedly sharp knife in the shape of a talon. He told his new wife that it was a symbol of Frith or familial peace and happiness between them and if he ever violated this Frith she could use the blade to do with him as she saw fit. The woman accepted this gift in the spirit in which it was meant.

All went well for a good number of years. That is, until the tribal chieftain's husband began to earn a considerable reputation for himself in warfare against other tribes. He began to become arrogant and at last began to view himself as the sole leader of his people. His advisors warned him against this behavior but he ignored them. At last he violated the trust of his wife by being publicly seen with other women.

'What happened then?' I asked.

Ari looked at me from across the fire. In the waning light of the late afternoon the flicker of the fire made his resulting smile look somewhat wolfish.

'She used the knife,' he said simply. 'It was her right to do so.'

He took the time to add another piece of wood to the fire. 'We are more civilized that that, of course, and with us the Frith-knife is a symbol that tells us that dishonorable behavior, particularly from males toward females, will not be tolerated. Nowadays, since the change to the Frith knife tradition, it tells us that proper respect is demanded from all by everyone within our circles.'

'I see. I will keep that in mind.'

'See that you do,' Ari said.

I spent the afternoon with Ari and we talked of many different things. Some were entirely mundane and covered everything from the lifestyle in the valley to politics and the weather. I could tell that Ari was trying to get an idea of the kind of a person I was, though I am sure he had already been given a fairly good picture by Agnes.

I had no problem with this. He was the master teacher, after all, and had been Agnes' Wataan in the tradition. He had every right to make sure that any new person hoping to learn would be a good fit for the ways he and Agnes walked.

'There are not many of us, though I hope that might change one day,' Ari said. He had suddenly changed subjects and had done it so fast that it completely caught me off guard. I sat there for a moment, looking at him strangely, then adapted to the shift in topic.

'Because we are small in numbers we have the advantage at this time to be very certain of the people we teach. One day we hope that many more will at least think about the Thornish ways because they are very Earth-friendly. For now we try to pass along what we know to a select few.' Ari paused for a moment and then said with a slight grin, 'You are apparently one of those.'

I said I was eager to learn and hoped to learn more from him as Agnes had suggested. To that he nodded again while poking at the fire with a stick.

'Well then, after we are done today I will send you back to Agnes' place. I assume you have time to spend up here in the valley so I'll tell you right now that if I do decide to teach you anything it will take about two weeks to give you the basics. If you are up for that we'll see what we can do.'

I told him I definitely had the time if he was willing to share with me.

Raven added another log to our fire and leaned back on his seat.

'Okay then,' he said. 'Has Agnes told you any of our foundation stories?' he asked.

'She told me one about Raven and his mate and how they came to this part of the world.' I replied. 'She told me how Raven came to the two tribes of men, the Native ones and the European settlers, the pagan settlers, and how Raven encouraged them to form a sacred band of brothers.'

'Raven and his wife Amber Eyes. Yes, that's a good story,' Ari said.

'Amber Eyes?' I asked.

'Didn't she tell you that?' Ari asked in surprise. I wasn't sure if he was joking with me or not.

'No, she didn't tell me that Raven's mate had that name.'

Ari rubbed his short goatee beard in consternation for a moment before looking back to me.

'Interesting. I wonder if she had a reason for that omission,' he said. 'No matter though, since you already know Amber Eyes anyway. After all, she sent you here.'

'Who...?' I began to ask, but then with a deep shiver that I could swear ran all the way from my toes to the top of my head I realized something. Several ideas suddenly flashed through my mind and for a brief second there in my memory was the face of the kindly old lady who had guided me so long ago in that café back east. I remembered her kindness and the amazing, warm, welcoming vibe she gave off and the dusky, black-haired young man who came to pick her up.

Her name had been Amber.

Could such a thing even be possible? My head was spinning. How did Ari even know about that? Had I mentioned Amber to Agnes? I couldn't remember even though I could clearly recall telling her about my meeting with Elizabeth in Calgary.

'How can any of that even be true?' I asked at last. 'How is such a thing possible?'

Ari's smile was genuine as he looked at me from his seat.

'Part of being Thornish is opening yourself up to such possibilities,' he replied. 'In the old times, the tribal people all over the planet believed in the innate ability of spirit people to change shape and do a lot of amazing things. They accepted these things because they saw them happen. It is a modern day curse when people don't trust their senses anymore. What we do here is to help people understand that they don't have to give in to the lies of so-called modern society anymore. We teach them to open up and turn on those old instincts.'

'It's pretty incredible,' I said at last.

'Life is pretty incredible, Carolyn,' Ari said. 'It is not this dull grey workaday world that a few power seekers have gotten everyone believing in. It is alive, vibrant and amazingly alive. You will begin to see this as you are shown more about our ways.'

'So…Amber was…?' I couldn't even bring myself to say the words.

Ari dismissed my continuing amazement with a casual wave of his hand.

'They are always doing things like that,' he said. 'So now I will tell you another of our tales and we'll see what you think of it. This one is called *Raven Visits the Thornwood.*'

* * *

Raven was flying along one day when he noticed, far, far below him, a very black, dark patch of forest. This was the deepest, blackest looking forest Raven had ever seen and in his long life he had seen many a forest from the air. Since Raven had always been attracted to mysterious things he decided to fly closer to see if he could find anything of interest.

As Raven flew closer he heard very faint sounds coming from down there in the black. It sounded to him like it might be singing of some kind. He wondered what kind of people would live in a forest so dark and like it enough to sing while they lived there, so he flew yet closer.

Eventually Raven flew so low that he found himself just above the tops of the highest trees. He went to land on one so he could rest and hear better but got a sudden surprise as he realized that these were no ordinary trees. They were ancient and sharp.

They were black thorn-trees. The whole forest, Raven realized as he looked for a softer perch and finally found one, was made up of these old, black thorn-trees. This made him even more curious about the kind of people who would possibly want to live down there among them.

Very curious now, Raven began to go lower into the forest. He hopped carefully from branch to branch, going into the dark beneath the canopy, avoiding the sharper places and all the while thanking the spirits (and his ancestors) that he had excellent night vision.

Eventually he managed to get to a place where he could see movement. He looked down and saw, still quite far below, a small encampment. There were three structures that looked like huts. They were round and possibly covered with hides of some sort. In the middle of the camp, surrounded by the three huts, a cheery-looking fire blazed and around this fire three shrouded figures sat. It was they who were the source of the singing Raven had originally heard.

Raven's curiosity drew him closer and closer to the ground until finally he found himself situated on a perch not much higher than the tops of the huts. Still, Raven was confident that he had not been detected by the mysterious human-looking shapes on the ground below him. After all, he knew that his night-black color and his stealth-skills would make him almost impossible to spot if he did not wish to be seen.

Raven had enough experience with human-people by now to recognize that although he could not understand the words of the song being sung below him (and he understood many languages including most human ones) he could tell that the song was being sung by females of the species. The song was very strange. It was slow and low and grim sounding for part of the time, and then it would rise to higher, lighter notes as it went on. Raven decided that he did not particularly like this song. It was not a happy song and he very much enjoyed happy songs.

What held his attention was the actions of the strange persons below him. They were all garbed in dark, hooded cloaks so he could see nothing of them as they sat there, save for their pale hands with long dexterous-looking fingers. Raven noticed that the three figures each had what looked like a small loom in their laps and they seemed to be weaving something out of a beautiful, sparkling silvery thread. The thread came from a large basket that sat to one side, by the fire. Also next to the fire was what looked like the stump of a log that was being used as a table top, and on this were scattered many small, brightly shining silver bits of something that looked like metal.

Raven could not tell exactly what those shiny things were but because he was intensely interested in shiny things he decided to sneak a little bit closer. As he hopped down to yet another level he could see that the small, silver things were small squares of metal and each one of these small shapes had symbols that he did not recognize engraved into it. Raven wondered if the strange, singing females would notice or even mind if he was to take one of the small pieces…just for luck?

And it was just as he was thinking these thoughts that something astonishingly fast caught his eye. As fast as he was, not even Raven could leap up and fly away in time. In seconds he found himself snared in a net of silver thread and dragged into the circle of the camp.

Raven looked out from the net in which he was caught. He tried to break free but the fine, yet incredibly strong threads held him fast. He looked upon the figures who had captured him and wondered what they could possibly gain from capturing him.

Under the hooded cloaks these females did not look like any of the other human people he had seen before. Their skin was very pale, almost silver-white like the light of the moon, and their hair, which they all wore long, was equally white. The eyes were slightly almond shaped and dark, very dark. They seemed like eyes that knew everything and that nothing could hide from.

All three of these strange beings were now gazing very intently upon Raven. They had stopped singing but they had not said anything.

Raven was becoming more and more uncomfortable with every moment and finally he spoke.

'I suppose you all know who I am,' he said, hoping to perhaps surprise them with the fact that he could speak.

They were not at all surprised and one of them even chuckled when he spoke.

'We know well who you are, Raven, son of Night,' she said in a voice that sounded not all that different from the strange song they had been singing.

'What shall we do with our little black-feathered spy, sisters?' another asked in that same strange, piping voice.

At last the third of the three females spoke.

'So, have you come to spy or to steal, Star-Farer? What is it you seek here?'

Raven tried to explain himself. He tried to make excuses and say that he had simply been curious.

'Yes indeed, you are the curious one,' she who had spoken first said.

'It is known too that you are an accomplished spy and sometimes a thief. Do you come to steal from us, Blade-of-the-Sky? Do you come to steal a glimpse of your destiny or is it something else?'

Raven explained that he had been drawn first by the mystery of the forest and then by the sound of their singing. He admitted that he had been intrigued by their weaving and by the small silver bits on top of the log.

Raven had spoken the truth and this seemed to satisfy them. It seemed that his instincts had proven correct and that those strange eyes could indeed see through any lies.

'You may not see your fate, Sun-Bringer,' the female that Raven had begun to think of as the 'middle sister' said. 'No one in mortal form may know this. I think you came here to snatch the runes you see there so that you could divine your wyrd.'

'No, nothing like that,' Raven said, by now feeling frightened. 'I like…shiny things is all.'

'He cannot help himself, sister,' said the first one to the middle sister. 'He is drawn not to the greater things but the smaller things.'

'I am still not sure of him,' said the third one. 'Perhaps we should teach him a lesson of some kind so he will not again try to sneak into our camp.'

'No, no lesson is necessary,' Raven said. 'If you were to be so kind as to release me I will be on my way with no difficulties.'

'There is indeed the possibility that we may let you go, Sky-Brother, but I think it would be rude of us to let you depart without a camp-gift from us to you.'

At this the three of them chuckled. It was not the most pleasant sound that Raven had ever heard and he detected the menace in it. He told them in his most polite voice that no gifting would be needed…that his freedom would be gift enough.

'Oh, but we insist,' said the first one. 'You must be aware of the rules of hospitality. What shall we give him so that he is reminded of us and our good manners?'

'I am still unsure of his motives,' said the third one. 'I still think that he may have come to steal a glimpse of Wyrd.'

Despite Raven's urgent assurances to the contrary the female closest to him urged him to be silent with her upturned finger. 'Shhh,' she said, and Raven was silent.

'No one should know the weave of their Wyrd,' she said after a moment. 'To know these kinds of things is a burden and a gift which we three alone fully carry. There are laws which bind even us and we must abide by them.'

'However, we perceive that you may be of use to us now. Since you so kindly decided to visit us we may make use of you,' said the middle sister.

'Sometimes knowledge is gentle,' said the first one.

'At other times it can be painful,' said the third one. 'But all knowledge is useful.'

And with that the three extended their hands toward Raven as he was held in the net. They did not touch him but he could feel the air grow colder with the closeness of their hands.

Raven felt fear as he had never felt fear before. He felt his casual, free attitudes retreating in the face of an ominous feeling that grew steadily stronger within him.

Suddenly, just as he was about to cry out and plead for mercy, the world around him changed. He was no longer in the camp in the forest but cast into a place out of a nightmare.

Raven was back in the air again, flying above the land. It was a sickly despoiled land that reeked of death and burned forests. The land was laid bare all around and he saw below him strange, tower-like structures clustered together. It was some kind of human habitation but the scale of it was huge. It looked to be constructed of some kind of stone. There was no green anywhere and the structures below him looked shattered and ruined. Black smoke billowed out of many of them.

The entire scene reeked of terror and death.

Raven flew on and saw beneath him a river…or what had been a river. It was now black with poison and it ran through a grove of fire-killed trees.

Everything was dead or dying. The feeling of nausea and despair overwhelmed him and he realized he had become sickly and weak. He went to seek a perch on one of the burned trees and as he did the entire tree crumbled to reeking ash beneath his feet.

Raven cried out in anguish.

And just as suddenly has he had been cast into that terrible nightmare world he found himself back in the circle of the three strange sisters.

He noticed that the silver net which had held him was no longer there. He had been freed at some point but he did not remember anyone removing the net.

Raven bowed his head before the three strange sisters and wept.

'It was so terrible,' he sobbed. 'Everything was dead or dying. The sacred was gone from the land. Please don't send me back there. I would surely die of sadness.'

For a moment there was a deep silence in that small circle around the fire. At last the third sister, the one which Raven had taken to be the eldest of the three, spoke.

'So you see this is our gift to you, Sable-Flame. We did not give it to you out of spite but rather out of kindness. We have seen that in a way you are lost and you need direction.'

'Now we have given you the seeds of a good and hale direction,' the middle sister added.

'I don't understand,' Raven said miserably.

What you have seen is what-may-be,' the first sister said quietly. 'In times ahead there will be many dire things brought to the Middle World through the acts of greedy human beings, terrible things unleashed upon the land so that a relative few might hold power. Eventually through this behavior all will die and this facet of the Middle World may be lost.'

'We give you the role of messenger,' the third sister said after a moment. 'Instead of living the carefree life of a trickster, spy and thief you may also now live the life of a noble teacher. We know you are fond of the humans. Go out and teach the few you find with unpoisoned hearts and clean minds. Teach them hale ways so that the thing you saw, the terror you experienced, may not be brought into the Middle World.'

Raven now wept uncontrollably.

'You have stolen my innocence,' he wept. 'I was never meant to have such knowledge.'

'Your destiny is still largely unwoven, Shadow-Flyer,' said the first sister, somewhat more kindly. 'Your innocence, as it is, is as intact as it was before you sought our camp. But now you know something that most others of any species do not know. You are armed with knowledge to help maintain the balance. Truly this is a gift, not a curse.'

'Difficult tasks are often born in the Thornwood,' the third sister said. 'But the things forged in this thorny darkness are often the strongest and the best able to serve the balance.'

And so it was that Raven was given knowledge of what might come to the Middle World if the ways of certain humans were allowed to prosper. Raven was released from the camp and the captivity of the strange cloaked sisters and he quickly made his way away from there.

It is said that on that fateful day Raven lost some of his innocence, yet he had the intelligence, the wisdom, and the drive, from that day forward, to carry the wisdom of the sacred balance out into the world of men.

* * *

'And so that is the story of Raven's visit to the Thornwood,' Ari concluded. 'You can make of it what you will but it is one of the foundational stories of our way. We believe that the folk of the Black Talon Society were given direction by Raven. Everything else has followed that in a good way.'

'It would explain why Raven and his mate came to the New World and why they spoke to those original tribesmen,' I said. 'Raven was doing his part to save the balance and his mate was helping him. He knew from the Wyrd sisters what could come in the future and so he was working to prevent that.'

'Yes, that is so,' Ari replied. 'It is also one of the reasons we took the term Thornwood to be our own. Nothing worthwhile is ever easy. In nature everything has a price and the prices exacted by the Thornwood can be steeper than most. It's a forge which produces finer steel in the end.'

Ari began talking about camping in the wild places. He spoke about survival and the need to have the basic skills in order to thrive out of doors.

'The most fundamental skill, one which most people seem to have lost these days, is respect. Everything in the world is alive, Carolyn Ravensdottir, everything has a spirit and many, many things are aware and conscious whether so-called science says so or not. The second basic skill is humility. When we go out in the world we need to stop having the arrogant conqueror attitudes because those don't work. We must be humble and know our place in the Middle World and elsewhere. Once we have re-learned these most basic skills we can talk about more advanced things like actually staying alive.'

I told him that I had learned a thing or two about that in my time and that Agnes had also taught me a lot.

'That's good because it saves me time,' Ari said. 'The core of the Thornish way is knowing how to survive in nature and, better than that, to thrive. Much of this knowledge has been stolen from the average person but to us they are second nature. The sacred balance is based in nature and in order for us to do our duty to the balance we work mostly in wild places. So during the next two weeks we will see where you are at and I will show you a thing or two to help you build your skills.'

So we sat there by the little fire in the stone-lined pit and talked. It was obvious to me that Ari was a man of vast experience and he had traveled the world seeking whatever wisdom he could gather. For a good portion of his life he had been a professional soldier and he had been very, very good at the trade.

However in his heart he said he had always been a man of knowledge and a seeker after the more arcane wisdom in the world. Working as a contractor allowed him to do a great deal of traveling and when he was not engaged in active duty he spent his time in libraries, museums and temples as well as examining a good many sacred sites and other places of mystery.

He shocked me by saying he had only lived in Pemberton about fifteen years or so. From his knowledge of the place and some of the things he said I assumed he had been here for much longer. Ari saw more than most people, much more, and because he 'got out in it' he developed a much more intimate connection with the land than most people did.

Ari seemed to have a stern, rugged exterior over top of what I sensed was a very deep, caring interior. I would even go so far as to describe him as being a very loving, sensitive person, but this was something that he never went to any lengths to share with me or anyone else I knew. Perhaps the hard exterior was a result of all of his years in the military, though I never knew for sure. What I do know is that as time passed and I got to know him better I understood that he was a passionate teacher and a good one.

I felt like I had barely sat down there by the fire and begun talking with this fascinating friend of Agnes' when I heard the sound of truck tires on gravel. Minutes later Agnes appeared and I realized that it was falling rapidly toward evening.

As Agnes approached and took note of the knife sitting in my lap she nodded to Ari respectfully and said something which sounded to me like the word 'meal.' I could not make it out and didn't want to ask directly.

Ari nodded back and said, 'You were right about Carolyn here. I think she has come to learn a few things from us.'

Then he turned to me and said, 'We were talking about survival and the skills a Thornish person needs to build as a basis for growth. Okay then, what I am going to do here is teach you a handful of things for now.'

Ari looked around for a moment and it almost seemed to me like he was a predator sniffing the wind. Whatever it was he had sensed was completely lost on me but I wondered if his tribal name, Raven, should have been Wolf instead.

Ari turned his attention back to me.

'I will begin teaching you these things tomorrow. Be here at 5:00 a.m. and come prepared to camp in the bush. Agnes knows what I mean and she'll get you straightened out. I'd invite you both to have dinner but that would just keep you up even later. Agnes knows what I can be like with late after-dinner chats.'

And with that we got up, said our farewells and left. Ari did not seem to be one who put a lot of effort into the ceremonies of greetings or farewells. When something was over it simply was. He didn't feel the need to 'fancy it up' as I had heard his friend Oliver once say.

So we said our brief goodbyes and before long were piled back in Agnes' beat-up Chevy truck on the road back down the valley.

'Can I ask you a question, Agnes?'

'Shoot.'

'When you came to pick me up you nodded at my knife and said 'meal.' What was that about?'

'You recall Ari said we have a culture, right? Well, what's culture without a language? We are a strange bunch, as you will discover, and a lot of what we have is derived from many other things over time, so there's a mixture of words and terms we use to communicate with each other. It's not really a language but more of a slang. We call it Thornish.'

'Makes sense…kinda.'

'Well, there are a good number of words and terms in our language. As you probably already noticed our lodge has a strong leaning toward a kind of northern European way. But there is also a strong feeling of respect for the Native ways and this land because obviously we aren't in northern Europe. In the past the Native people of these North American lands gave our people a lot of gifts and since most of us live here in North America we also honor the ways of this land.'

'I remember the story about Raven's gift,' I said. 'Ari told me another one today. Things are starting to make sense.'

'There are influences from different cultures here,' Agnes continued. 'These all come from members who have come in over the years, especially the guys who founded the Lodge who were a mixture of Indians, Germans, Northmen and English. So the Thornish we use reflects that. It has just developed that way over the years. There is no particular rhyme or reason to it…it just is.'

She smiled. 'The word you heard me use, by the way, was *miyos*,'

Agnes said, pronouncing it 'mee-osh.' 'We use it kind of like we would say 'good' in English. There are a number of words that can be used but miyos is one of them.'

And so we continued into the dusk, in relative silence. I realized that I was quite tired and would welcome the coming sleep.

8. The First Four Shields

The next morning Agnes dropped me off in front of Ari's house. It was dark and windy and quite chilly and it looked as though we might get a bit of rain. Autumn was in full tilt and I could smell the scent of falling and dying leaves.

Agnes did not stay around but helped me get my backpack and some other gear she had lent me out of the bed of the pickup, and was off on her way. 'Good luck!' she said, rather ominously, waving as she drove away.

Ari standing in the yellow rectangle of light of his front doorway. 'Coffee's on,' he said.

As I sat down at the table in Ari's large, utilitarian-looking kitchen, the first thing I saw was a beautifully made leather sheath. It looked like it was made out of some kind of well-oiled heavy belt leather. It had a little row of fringe hanging from it and these were beaded with black and red glass beads. It was a very pretty sheath and I had a good idea, since it was empty, what it was for.

'Yeah, that's for you,' Ari said as he brought cups and the coffee pot over to the table. 'I threw it together last night. You can't be walking around the woods with a bare blade stuck in your belt.'

I went to the living room, got the knife he had given me out of my pack, and tried it in the sheath. I was not surprised when it fit perfectly.

'Red and black are Thornish colors,' he said. 'Red is for blood and for power and for what we call Bloodfire, the heart of the Thornish warrior. Black is for the Black Root of knowledge and the deeps of night, where all power and all life is born.'

'Thank you. It's very pretty.' It was all I could think of to say.

Ari gave me a kind of sour look, which was quite funny. 'Pretty, eh?' he said. 'Maybe not the word I would use to describe it, but okay. Glad you like it.'

Ari poured the coffee, which was hot, black and very fragrant. He also brought over a small tray that held a bowl of brown sugar and a container of honey with spoons. He went to the fridge and retrieved a glass bottle of milk as well.

'Hope you don't mind that I don't have any white sugar. I can't stand that stuff. Rots the teeth and the brain too.'

I had no problem with that. I poured myself a cup and added a bit of milk.

'Not a sweetener kind of gal?' He smiled. 'I like you already.'

We sat there for a few moments simply enjoying our coffee. The brew was very strong but I kind of liked it that way. Back in Ontario I had been a fan of the lighter, more sweetened beverages, yet during my time on the road, where black coffee was a common form of human-fuel, I had adapted.

I really liked the overall vibe of Ari's house. In some ways it had a very similar feel to Oliver's house. It had a deeply warm, lived-in, welcoming feeling. Ari's house also had a more mystical feeling that was hard to describe, although maybe I was reading more into it because of something Agnes said the evening before.

I had asked Agnes what Ari might have to teach me and she had been reluctant to go into any detail. She told me that although she and Ari were both Thornish, they approached the way of the Black Root somewhat differently.

The *Black Root* is what Thornish people consider to be the First

Knowledge or First Wisdom that was passed down to humankind when we were originally created. Thornish people believe that in the old times humans had a much more complete grasp of this knowledge than we do today and that much has been lost due to so-called civilizing influences. A large part of the Thornish way is expressed in the manner each individual relates to the Black Root and the never-ending quest of learning more from it.

Agnes concluded by saying that in mundane, commonly understood terms her own practice could be seen as being roughly analogous to that of a country witch, a herbalist and a healer who spent a good deal of time learning about plants and such, and who spent a good deal of time Faring into the world of spirit to learn more.

She then told me while she and Ari shared the Thornish path, there were also ways they differed. Ari walked a much more grim and possibly darker trail than she did. His was the Warrior way and he had endured much hardship and pain on his path to deeper understanding.

'Ari is a powerful psychic, if I can use that term,' Agnes said finally. 'His gifts simply blow mine straight out of the water and I'm certainly no push-over. He is slightly telepathic too as anyone who knows him will tell you. My Hearth-brother is a very powerful man, Carolyn, and he is really good at concealing 99% of that from anyone on the outside. He walks some very dark roads and has friends in places of spirit where even I wouldn't dare go. I guess you could call him a Thornish mage if you had to drop a label on him, but because our ways are unique even that label doesn't really fit.'

When we arrived back at her house she showed me her own Frith-knife and told me hers had also been a gift from Ari. Its blade was very similar to mine but the handle was different. It was stained blood red and carved with many tiny black runes and sigils.

'Notice how when he made your Frith-knife he used a very light finish on the haft? It's more light orange than anything else and there are no runes. Well, he did that because he already has a better idea of what you are capable of than you do – maybe than you ever will. Figuring that out will be a big part of your journey and as to the runes or sigils, I think you will have to add those yourself, just as I did.'

These things were going through my mind when I found myself once again in Ari's house. I knew there were many preconceived ideas I had to get rid of when it came to understanding the worlds of magic and of spirit. I certainly saw no magical circles or arcane equipment hanging around his home.

'You said you were going to teach me some things?' I asked Ari over the rim of my coffee cup.

Now Ari smiled. He was capable of some very bright, beautiful smiles when he allowed himself. His eyes, which were bright blue, like bits of glacier ice, only added to the sunshine when he smiled. I didn't feel like I was in the presence of some big, bad magician, but there was a tiny voice in the back of my head that warned me to maintain respect and manners in his presence.

'Yes indeed,' he said. 'I will teach you a few things. As Agnes probably told you, she sees you having a destiny that will take you off of her beaten path. She wants you to learn these foundations from me because she thinks you will learn better from a Spearman than from a Farer.'

A Spearman in the Thornish context is a person who walks the darker roads of the Thornwood and who often goes through harder ordeals and deals with nastier beings along that road.

I had seen the sacred stang Agnes kept in a special 'working room' in her house. Her stang was one of her prized possessions: a six foot long wooden branch with two very sharp tines on one end. It was made from hazel, she told me, a gift from a dear departed friend, and Agnes had shaped the wood herself. The stang was oiled a deep reddish brown color and was covered in runes, sigils and small inset red and black stones. Near the top, just under where the tines began, there was a band of red leather cord from which hung crow feathers and glass beads. It was very beautiful.

Agnes explained that there were different paths within the Thornwood and initiates walked their own path as their destiny guided them. There were generally two categories, the Spear-folk and the Farer-folk. For the most part the Farer-folk took the stang as their symbol and the Spear-folk took an edged implement, usually a spear, as their tool of choice.

'What I will teach you first will be the Six Shields,' Ari said from across the table. 'The Six Shields are skills which will protect you and help you to feel at home in the wilderness. They are the basis of what I have come to call Ullr's Road. I use that term in reference to the old Norse God, Ullr, who is a god that watches over hunters and wilderness travelers.'

'Oo-ler?' I asked, pronouncing this strange-sounding word for the first time.

'Ullr is very ancient,' Ari explained. 'Primordially so. He was said to be ancient even before the time of the other gods and goddesses. He is an Elder Kin who is much closer to the First Knowledge of the world, I think.'

Ari paused for a moment before continuing.

'You will come to know that among the Thornish folk there are many unique ways to walk one's path. Although the basis of the way is a convergence of northern European and Native ways, the European influence is probably the more obvious one. Both are equal and have much to teach but you will see the influences in each person's unique ways. My own reflects what I was taught as a boy. I never knew the taint of monotheistic thinking. I was taught about the old ways and of the gods and goddesses of northern Europe. Ullr has always been very good to me and I honor him for that.'

'Are all of these Elder Kin, these gods and goddesses, based in the Norse ways?' I asked. I had asked similar questions of Agnes but for some reason she had not given me a clear answer on the subject.

'No,' Ari replied. 'I have a special relationship with some of the Elder Kin of that culture. I am part Native by blood but also part northern European and while I have learned so much from my Native brothers and sisters my primary road lies in my northern European roots.'

Ari looked at me for a long moment in silence.

'The Thornish way is always looking for the thing we call the Black Root, the First Knowledge. That means we are always seeking the deepest, most primal ways and the most ancient of understandings. When we go that far back we see things differently and we realize while there are many beings that humans might call gods or goddesses there have also been numerous names for a good portion of them. We are animists; we believe everything has spirit, and we believe that there are beings out there, greatly advanced over us, who have involved themselves with the affairs of the Middle World. There are many names for these folk and yes, some of them may sound familiar from time to time.'

Ari then explained the nature of each of the Six Shields.

The First Shield was the self. It was concerned with becoming friends and allies with oneself. Ari explained that most people in modern times often had an uneasy alliance or sometimes even hatred held within each individual. Until a person can come to grips with and learn to trust oneself there can be little progress.

The Second Shield was the craft of shelter. Ari taught me that when a person is out in the wild it is always good to have shelter. This shelter can not only protect a person against the elements but it can also provide a powerful psychological and spiritual tool with which a person can survive even the harshest conditions.

The Third Shield was Fire. Ari taught that the fire-people are very much alive and conscious and they have long had a generally friendly relationship with human beings. The teachings of the Third Shield were centered around fire and the making and maintenance of fires.

The Fourth Shield was Water. Water is deeply sacred and human beings require water to survive. In a situation out in the wild, Ari taught, it is important to have access to clean water.

The Fifth Shield is the teaching of food gathering in the wild. As Ari spoke about this Shield I could tell that it was something especially sacred to him. He told me of how he had, as a boy, dedicated himself to the teachings of Ullr and how that Elder Kin, as well as many other helpful spirit people, had shown him many powerful things over the years. He emphasized several times during this initial talk how deeply sacred the acquisition of food was and how it was so very important for Thornish people to never, ever take their food for granted.

'Every single thing we put into our bodies dies so that we can carry on,' he said, quite emotionally. 'Eating is a holy act because you are being trusted to carry the life-energy of those who died so you can live. You are carrying them with you and a piece of everything you will ever consume stays with you in spirit.'

Finally, Ari spoke of the Sixth Shield, which was centered on the aspects of spirit when one is out in the wild. Without proper respect for the world of spirit, he said, there can be no true experience and learning.

'We will go out into the green and teach you and test you and in the end we will see whether you are more comfortable with a spear or a stang in your hands,' Ari said.

He asked if I had eaten and I told him that I had. He then asked me to bring in my backpack and we went through it to see if I had everything I would need. We spent about an hour there in his kitchen, sorting through things and rearranging my backpack, and in the end he was satisfied.

'We will be out for twelve days,' he said finally, he saw the astonished look on my face. 'Didn't Agnes tell you anything about her first teachings with me?'

'She didn't tell me she was out in the bush in autumn for nearly two weeks, no.'

'Well, we will not be in the bush for all of that time. Just trust in me, young learner, and we shall see what we shall see.'

Ari went to the large frame pack leaning against the wall near the back door and hoisted it on his back.

'Eventually we get to the point where we need to pack very little or even nothing with us when we go into the green,' he said. 'However, you are new to this and the fall is here as well. We want to travel as lightly on the land as we can. Many of our relations are going to sleep this time of year so we want to disturb them as little as possible.'

With that he walked out the door. I took my own pack and followed him.

'Don't you want to lock your back door?' I asked. I was concerned that someone might break into his home if we were going to be gone so long, yet I almost immediately thought better of it. After all, I was speaking to someone who was apparently a kind of sorcerer.

Ari waved his hand in a gesture of light-hearted dismissal.

'No, it will be fine,' he said. 'Just make sure the latch clicks, will you? One time I came back and found my big brother sitting in my living room. He made a hell of a mess and tore up my couch.'

'Your older brother wrecked your living room?'

Ari looked at me quite seriously and said, 'No, I mean that a big black bear found his way in, raided my cupboards and then ate part of my couch…which is why I find that if I make sure all the doors are at least latched there is less chance of that.'

'Oh,' I said. It was all I could think of to say. I pulled the kitchen door shut and it clicked as the latch fell into place.

I hoped we would not come back to a large bear in the house. A moment later, looking back on what I thought might be the last sign of civilization I would ever see, I followed my newest teacher into the woods.

* * *

I will not go into fine detail about the adventures I had out in the forest during that time. Since I am writing this so that someday others might find their way to a similar path, I will keep it simple. I also have concerns about giving too much away at this point. I remember what Agnes said about layers of knowledge and some things must be earned in order to be truly appreciated. I will tell something of what happened during that trip so I can give the reader an idea of those basic teachings.

On the first day, as we went into the woods, the going was quite easy. I walked alongside Ari and mostly listened as he pointed out various plants, animals and features of the forest to me. At about a half an hour along, he motioned me to walk quietly and slow down. Moments later we watched as two female deer made their way across the trail and into deeper bush.

Once the deer were gone we continued along for some time. Eventually the trail became steeper and I realized just how out of shape I was. I set myself to do it, though, and concentrated on getting up the steep incline that we were walking on, focusing on two things; my feet on the ground and the occasional sound of Ari telling me some interesting fact or another.

After a time the trail evened out and when I looked up we were approaching a small clearing in which a cute little dome-shaped hut had been built. It had been made with branches from local trees and covered over with brush and old oiled canvas tarps. It looked almost medieval actually and for a moment I thought of the Tale of Raven in the Thornwood. I wondered if the huts of the Wyrd sisters had looked anything like this.

Ari set down his pack and hauled a few items out. He put these supplies inside the hut.

'This is your home for the next three nights. I won't be far off but don't expect to see me till sunup on the third day. You have firewood and water so there is no reason to leave the camp.'

Even though Agnes and Ari had both told me there would be ordeals of a sort, this was a surprise to me. 'What am I supposed to do here then, meditate?' I asked.

Ari nodded. 'The idea is that you need a bit of time to get to know yourself. So the next little while will be all about getting to know Carolyn. Meditate on that, think on it and see what you come up with. It's a long road for many but it's a good beginning.'

I nodded in understanding.

'If I may ask, what has Agnes taught you about the Vörd?' he asked.

Vörd is another one of those Thornish terms Agnes taught me. At first I had a bit of difficulty keeping track of the various words and concepts but over time they became more familiar.

'You might be wondering, hey, why bother using these made up or borrowed terms when we can just be normal and use everyday words that might mean the same thing?' Agnes told me once. 'I know I have spoken about this before but it bears repeating. Repetition and teaching, you know the drill by now.' She paused for a moment, then continued. 'Well, my friend, there are two important reasons for all of this. One is that some of the terms are used to describe things that have no exact analogy in normal English and the other reason, probably the more important of the two, is that language is culture.'

She emphasized that last bit, the language-is-culture part, and further explained that the Elders who founded the Thornish ways realized that they were indeed creating culture.

'Thornish ways need to be free to grow on their own, unchained to other ways,' Agnes said. 'And so having our own terms and words …it's almost a dialect now…helps us to remember that we are, in fact, a kind of pagan culture unto ourselves. Some of the words are borrowed, some are created for a specific use, and some come to us from experiences in the spirit world. We make no apologies for it and it works well for us.'

We talked about the Vörd quite early on and why it was important to Thornish people. A Vörd is a kind of helper from the spirit world, a being that has a foot in both worlds. Every living thing has a spirit and among humans there is a nature-spirit that comes into us the very day we are born. Some suggest that this spirit is a part of us even before birth, that it is a connection to the Great Essence and the Black Root.

This spirit creature watches over us and guides us throughout our lives. Some people lose their spirit creature and when that happens they might become sick. At other times a spirit creature may feel mistreated or become bored and leave the person they were with, and the person may become sick or mentally or spiritually unbalanced. Thornish people think it is very important to get to know one's spirit-creature or Vörd, as it is called. It is believed that when one gets to know their Vörd they can have a much better, happier, healthier life and grow in wisdom and power.

I had spent some time under Agnes' teaching trying to make a connection with my Vörd. I had a very strong feeling that a raven was watching over me and had experienced this feeling many times in my life. I had also known for a long time that ravens and crows often felt little fear around me and were attracted to me. I have had a great many dreams in my life involving such birds.

Yet, as Agnes had said to me, the Vörd is not something you pick because you like it or it is cool or something. The Vörd picks you and has in fact picked you before you were born. So it is best to open oneself up to the possibility that your Vörd may not be the specific creature you imagine it to be.

'Open yourself up when you are in the silent place or the places of power in nature,' Agnes told me. 'When you are really humble and you allow yourself to really truly give thanks for everything around you, and thanks to your Vörd for all the things he or she has given you over the years, you will get to know your spirit-friend quite powerfully. Think of it like a Hollowing that you experience all of the time. It's important never to lose the reverence.'

'I have done a bit of work with the Vörd,' I said now to Ari. 'Agnes and I have been working on that together.'

In the Thornish way of speaking there are often a lot of words that are the same in singular as they are in plural. A person doesn't say Vörds if they are referring to more than one, but simply says Vörd.

'Well, here is another opportunity for you to think about that,' Ari replied. 'Take the time to open yourself up to the Vörd and if you are balanced you will learn a lot.'

Ari hesitated for a moment, then reached into his pocket and handed me a small leather bag.

'Flint and steel,' he said. 'Get a head start on that Third Shield if you want. Try to get a fire started without using a lighter or matches. You know how to start a fire, don't you?'

I had at least done that. Quite a few times in my life I had started campfires and fires in fireplaces. I was glad I had, otherwise I might have had some difficulties. I nodded.

'Good,' he said. 'I figured that Agnes would have told me if there was any critical skill you were lacking.'

And with that he simply hoisted his pack and walked away, toward a trail on the other side of the clearing. With little else to do I put my pack down and crawled inside the hut.

The first day passed without incident. I was actually quite glad to have the day to myself and the place was very peaceful. I lit a fire using only the flint and steel Ari had given me. It was a bit of a challenge but I felt a deep satisfaction when I was finally successful.

Afternoon faded into night and before long I was sitting alone just outside the door to the little hut before my crackling fire. I spent the time in meditation and deliberately chose not to eat. Ari left me some supplies, which I had stored in the hut, but I figured I might have a better go of things if I had a clear mind. Food digestion can lead to fuzzy thinking as far as I am concerned.

The first night passed peacefully and the next day I puttered about the camp, looking for things to do. The night before I tried to focus on getting to know myself better, thinking good thoughts and even talking to myself quite a bit. I hoped that there were no spirit people around who saw me doing this and thought I was nuts.

The second day I continued to talk to myself and think about how I could be a better friend and ally to myself. This was not as easy as I thought it would be. I wished there had somehow been more instruction given by either Agnes or Ari on this one.

The second evening came and with it a storm. It rained like crazy and I found myself stuck in the hut without a fire. I huddled in the dark in my sleeping bag with the extra blanket I had been given. I spent a long time just sitting there looking out on the hammering rain, listening to the wind in the trees and cradling my Frith-Knife in my hands.

'Remember,' Ari's voice came to my mind, a memory of the first day I spent at his home. 'Frith is the sacred peace of the hearth and camp and held between hale folk. The Frith-knife is a symbol of that peace and a warning to those who might not respect it.'

Just holding the knife in its beaded sheath gave me a deep sense of comfort. It helped me feel as though I was doing something good, that I was on the right path. The right path for me, anyway.

The morning of the third day I crawled out of the hut to find Ari sitting on a rock tending to a newly-kindled fire. I was really surprised to find him there. Didn't he say he would be back for me in three days? Had three days passed already and I didn't notice? Had I somehow missed an entire day?

I hadn't heard a thing but was roused by the faint smell of wood smoke. Unlike the night before the sky above was clear and blue and it looked like everything was already drying out a bit.

Ari was roasting two nice trout on a makeshift spit over the fire. I had no idea where he had gotten the fish from but it smelled delicious.

It wasn't long before I had a plate of fish and a steaming cup of joe handed to me and I realized that over the past two days I had taken only water. The food was amazing and so was the coffee.

'I didn't eat at all over the past two days,' I told Ari. 'I figured it might help me have a clear mind. You know, it was a nice time but it seemed uneventful.'

Ari looked at me thoughtfully.

'It is a tiny step, my friend,' he said. 'You have opened a small crack in the door. Do this again a few more times and you will see progress. This is just to show you how it's done. That's why I came back today rather than tomorrow. Just checking in on you.'

I suspect he was watching me from a distance to make sure I was okay all the while—or some of the time at least. He probably reappeared more to give me the feeling I was watched over and I really appreciated his efforts. Even in this short time with him I was starting to think of Ari as an elderly uncle rather than simply a friend of a friend.

Ari brought out a bag with more supplies in it, mostly dried fruit and beef jerky. He said he did not intend for me to be out here fasting but rather learning as deeply as I could with the skills I currently had.

An hour later, after we finished the fish and coffee, Ari stood up.

'I am never far off but I am glad to see you have been okay thus far on your own. I'll leave you for one more night now, so try to enjoy yourself and remember, become part of the experience, don't just relate to it as an outsider.' And with that, just like before, he simply grabbed up his pack and left.

I settled into life in my camp for one more day. I worked hard at opening up more to the experience as Ari suggested and I realized that letting go of many of my preconceptions about reality was not as difficult as I originally thought. This probably had a lot to do with spending time in the wild places, which makes it easier to let go of all the human-made constructs we live with. I fed the little fire with sticks I found in the area and spent the afternoon sitting by the fire and trying to be a part of the landscape.

The day went much quicker than the previous ones and by the time the sun was setting behind the mountains in the west I was marveling at how fast the time went by. Nighttime soon followed and I went to my blankets inside the hut with a deep feeling of peace.

The morning of day four found me crawling out of the hut sometime after sunrise. As I had expected, Ari was sitting nearby tending the small fire. This time he was not cooking but he did have a small pot of steaming water on the rocks in case I wanted instant coffee or tea. I greeted him and gratefully took the offered cup of instant coffee in my chilled hands.

He told me that today would probably be a good day to start with dried meat, rather than cooking anything fancy. He handed me a good-sized chunk of jerky. It was a very dark color and had a really great, rich taste.

'Moose,' he explained after seeing the expression on my face. 'From last season. As always, a sacred gift.'

A half an hour later we were packed up and ready to go. I made sure the small fire was completely extinguished before we left and checked around to make sure that, other than the hut and the fire pit, there was no sign I had been there.

Before we left Ari pulled a cloth bag out of his coat pocket.

He handed it to me. 'In our tradition everything has spirit, everything is alive. We live in balance with all of these many beings who live around us and to show our respect we leave offerings.'

I looked in the bag and saw it contained a mixture of tobacco and white sage, with seeds and dried berries mixed in. Ari also handed me a small pile of copper pennies.

'We give a lot of different kinds of things in offering,' he said. 'Whatever we can spare. It's giving something back to the spirits of the land so there are nuts and seeds there for the little four-leggeds and the birds.'

'And the pennies?'

'I find that the land wights or land spirits sometimes like them. Have you heard of Dwarves? They are not what you might think. They are deep dark workers of the land and rock and they really like metals, pure metals, not junk metals, so if you offer pennies you are making a good trade for future favors or generally good luck.'

So I went to several places along the perimeter of the camp and left small piles of offerings and a few pennies. I offered silent thanks to the spirit people for letting me stay in that place and I hoped they might allow me to return there again one day.

I returned Ari's offering bag to him, thinking I would have to make a bag of my own like that. Agnes had shown me the way of offerings at the many little shrines she had inside and outside of her home and I gave myself a bit of a hard time for not thinking about making offerings out in the wild. I put making and filling an offering bag of my own on my to-do list.

On the afternoon of that fourth day, after we walked for at least ten miles, we came into a section of really deep pine and fir woods. The woods were quite dark as many of the trees in there were very large and old, casting deep shadows. In we went along a very faint trail I didn't even see until Ari turned off onto it without hesitation. It looked at first like it a game trail, the kind of path made by deer. As we walked deeper into the artificial dusk created by the trees the trail became a little wider and a little more worn.

At last we came to another clearing. There was something about this clearing I didn't like. I couldn't place the origin of the feeling but it was there, just beyond the dark circle of trees. I felt kind of like there was something watching me. It didn't seem menacing in any way but it was also not particularly welcoming either.

Ari stopped and set his pack down beside the small central fire pit that looked as though it had not seen use in many years. Leaves and dead pine needles were everywhere in the clearing and had filled the small, blackened pit with its ring of rounded stones.

'This is a very special place,' Ari said at last. 'It's a hard teacher but I think you can handle what it has to pass along.'

'I'll be honest with you and say I don't really like the feel of this place. Gives me the willies.'

Ari nodded. 'Well, maybe that is because the spirits who live around here don't like strangers all that much. Maybe it's because this little place is pretty far off the beaten track and they don't get a lot of outsiders in here. Maybe they are waiting to see what you will do once I leave you here on your own.'

'I am not sure if that is such a good idea,' I said. I felt a creeping sense of fear rising through my body and I wondered if my staying around here might just make any local spirit people all the angrier.

'You know, back in the day when I did this kind of thing it was a lot tougher than it is today. We had to be more secretive and in the area where I was taught it was not quite as easy to find isolated places like this, places where no one would come stumbling through.'

'Or maybe like places where the body would never be found,' I said, only half joking.

'Carolyn, we are here to talk about the Second Shield, which is also called the Second Grandfather by some. You probably know what I am going to say next.'

'The Second Shield is the way of shelter?'

'Yes,' he said. 'And by shelter I mean that we are talking about things that can shelter your body from the elements and such, but to a Thornish person this means a whole lot more.'

Ari sat down on the ground by the fire and motioned me to do the same.

He explained that it was the desire of Thornish people not to isolate themselves from the elements so much as to embrace them. Yet it was also understood that there were times when the somewhat frail limits of the human body meant that physical shelter was required in order to survive. Beyond that, however, the folk of the Thornwood also sought to create spaces where they could shelter themselves mentally and spiritually if need be, such as on a retreat for ritual or simply for silent meditation. Again he emphasized that those who were of his tradition didn't want to cut themselves off from spirit, it was just that sometimes it was necessary to shield oneself from things that might be distractions to one's work.

'Now here in this place there are some spirit folk who don't like strangers. You were very right in picking that up, Carolyn. I am glad to see that you have sharp senses. Not everyone would have been able to pick up on that.'

Ari then told me that there was another reason for the perceived animosity I felt. He told me how many, many years earlier some white men had been logging in the area and that this logging had made the local Indians upset because they considered the area to have special significance. The local Native folk were ignored and the white men cut most of the trees down. Near the end of the cut there was a fire in the logger's camp that pretty much destroyed the rest of the timber for a good distance around. It was also said that several people got themselves killed in that fire. Over the decades the forest had been rebuilding itself. It was building back its former good *Medicine* as Ari called it, and the forest was always unsure when people came around that it did not know.

I asked Ari if we were on Indian land and he just laughed and told me that everywhere we go is on Indian land. He added that he was known to Elders in the area and he had long ago been given permission to be where we were.

Ari went off into the woods at various places and brought back several fallen bits of wood, branches and scrub. He made a big pile of this stuff at one end of the clearing.

With a stick he drew a number of pictures of different types of shelter on the dirt. One was a simple lean-to-like affair that had a square stick frame on one side with more branches angling down at a 45 degree angle. Another was a single log laid at an angle against the top of a stump or fallen tree with smaller branches laid against it so that it looked kind of like a fish backbone with the ribs sticking out. A third design was shown with a larger number of sticks laid at about a 45 degree angle against the bole of a live tree.

'All of these are covered with brush, leaves, whatever you can find,' he said. 'In summer you want about six inches or less coverage because you are mainly trying to stay out of the wind or rain. In winter you might want to have an arm's length worth of thickness for insulation. Another one you can do is to simply lean branches against a fallen log and cover the thing up with leaves and bark—whatever gets the job done.'

Ari explained that there were many more designs, probably dozens more, for simple shelters but the idea was to work with what was at hand and get sheltered as soon as possible. What mattered was that one could make a shelter and that the shelter would be in balance with the local environment.

'If you have a good oilskin or a tarp, use that as well,' he added and mentioned, as he had already done several times, that he had little use for the plastic or nylon tarps he was seeing in use. There was a kind of unhealthy energy with them and things like that, if ever lost or left in the bush, would take a very long time to decompose. Instead he taught it was better to use as many natural things as possible so that a better feeling of balance would be achieved.

'Staying dry and warm is important but not as important as remaining in balance. When a person is in balance, you'd be surprised at what they are capable of. In a survival situation it is no different.'

'You spoke about a spiritual aspect?' I asked.

'Oh yeah,' he said, and began rummaging around in his pack. 'I figure that since you are not simply some kid come out here to learn a few camping skills but are in fact hoping one day to be initiated, I would show you another level to this.'

Ari brought out a canvas bag and handed it to me. 'Sometimes we need to find a way to shelter ourselves on different levels than just the physical,' he said.

I opened the drawstrings of the bag and looked inside. There was an orange-yellow powder in there that smelled quite familiar.

'Cornmeal, salt, ashes and a bit of mugwort, sweetgrass and sage,' Ari said in answer to my questioning look. 'You will find that Thornish people will have on hand a good number of things that come from the worlds of folk magic. This is a somewhat mild mixture we can use for warding. We can set up a protective boundary with it to show our intent to certain folk who might want to interfere with us. It can be used for rituals or for simple ease of mind when we are meditating or seeking peace in other ways. It works quite well.'

Ari explained that in matters of spirit, ritual and magic, in the Thornish way at least, will is very important, as is intent. If a person came with respect and went about their business with a powerful will and intent, if one had focus and determination, then one could accomplish great things.

'By itself the mixture in that bag is useful, but if you use it with the three sisters I spoke of, Will, Intent, and Respect, you will greatly magnify its abilities as you will magnify your own.'

I thought about various things I learned from Agnes and indeed, one of them was the setting of protective barriers during some kinds of ritual work. She explained to me that for the most part the barrier was an aid to the practitioner as it helped them form mental imagery with regard to the work ahead. However, in the case of some wights, the material used in such barriers could have a very real effect.

Ari started placing items back in his pack but left me with the bag in my hand. I suddenly realized we had been sitting there discussing the building of shelters for a good number of hours. My hands were sore from all of the brush I had been sorting through and from the contact of chilled wood on partially numb fingers.

'So think of this as a test of skill,' he said. 'You have pretty much everything you need to make any of the shelters we discussed. Feel free to build a fire too if you want to, but I will warn you that it can get pretty chilly here in this wood at night. It's fall, so you don't have to worry too much about any four-leggeds coming by…well, maybe not Bear anyway.' He chuckled and handed me a sizable ball of rough-looking twine. 'Here's a cheater for you in case you decide on the lean-to design.' And with that, Ari got up and hoisted his pack back on his shoulder.

'A test of my skills?' I said, still very unsure of myself.

'You have done very well so far, Carolyn,' he said. 'The path is useless if we hand you everything. And yes, everything in life is a test. I will see what you can come up with when I come back here tomorrow morning.'

Ari walked a few paces and then turned to face me once again. 'And it's worth mentioning that I've seen you're not all that afraid to be out in the bush by yourself,' he said. 'You have no idea how rare that is in people nowadays, so you have earned respect in that as well.' He smiled and turned back to the trail.

I watched him go. Once again he left by a different way than the one we had come in. I wondered where he went when he left me on my own.

One thing I realized when I was first left out in the area of the little hut was that if I busied myself I would feel less anxious about being alone out in the woods. So I started to get busy…but then I realized that if the local spirit people were uneasy the best thing to do would be to speak to them and leave them signs of my respect.

So I did that. Ari had left the small offering bag and I took it up and went to the edges of the clearing. I spoke to the spirit people as if I were speaking to respected elders. I spoke deliberately and as politely as I could. I told them who I was and why I was there in that place. I also told them that I wanted to be on good terms with them if that was something they would permit. Then I left offerings, little piles of the tobacco mixture, and some of the remaining pennies.

It seemed to me as though the feeling of odiousness eased a little after I left the offerings and said my words. I wasn't sure if this was my imagination or something else but I determined to be as respectful as possible.

I took what I felt I would need from the pile of materials and built the simplest of the designs I could manage. I ended up putting together a very shoddy-looking lean-to held together with lengths of twine. This I covered over with as much brush as I could find. The whole process took me about two and a half hours but I wasn't entirely sure about this, since Agnes discouraged me from bringing along a watch.

In the end I stood some distance away and looked at my creation. I was less than impressed and hoped it would not collapse on me during the night. I also hoped it wouldn't rain.

In the interests of safety I decided not to have the shelter too close to the fire pit. I knew I would have to grope my way to the shelter after dark but that was okay with me.

I cleaned out the fire pit and refilled it with the basic bits of wood I would need to get a fire started. As I had been taught I brought only the tiniest twigs and dried leaves into the pit in the beginning. To these I added tiny shreds of dried bark I found lying around.

I also decided not to use the cornmeal mixture. I didn't throw down a circle or try to create any sort of line between myself and the rest of the world. I trusted the local spirits and did not wish to offend them by creating any kind of barrier between us.

As night came I was very tired both physically and mentally. I had been though a lot over the past months and especially over the past few days with Ari, and I just needed to sleep.

'Here I am, a young woman alone out in the middle of the bush, living in a shelter that might fall on me any second and worried about whether the local spirits might have it in for me,' I said aloud to myself and to anyone else who might happen to be listening. 'But ya know what? I am no threat to anyone around here and way too tired to stay stressed about it.'

And with that I crawled into the little shelter, burrowed under the pile of blankets Ari had been kind enough to leave me, and, despite the cold, I gave in to the peace of sleep.

The very first thing Ari asked me the next morning, when I found him sitting by my small and now rekindled fire, was if I had been warm enough.

Even though we were having somewhat of a mild spell weather-wise, I told him I had never really been what I could call comfortable. Between the hard ground and the chill seeping in I admitted that I missed the little well-insulated hut I had been in earlier.

Ari nodded toward my makeshift shelter and told me that my skills needed work.

I didn't say what was on my mind, but I feel it is important to note that throughout my journey with Ari I always had a feeling of confidence that my latest teacher was never all that far away. I never imagined myself as being truly alone in the woods. I knew that for my own safety, and probably his own peace of mind with a newcomer, Ari had not been all that far away from me when I camped. It was this feeling of security that played a big part in allowing me to actually sleep on those initial nights on my own.

Ari had breakfast cooking on a makeshift spit by the time I woke up. This time there were several grouse sizzling away like small chickens as they warmed over the fire.

'Don't expect that you will always wake up to food,' Ari said after I told him that the meat smelled delicious. 'But I like to see the student focusing on the skill I am teaching them, not so much on their growling stomach. Later you will get your own food or bring it with you.'

We spent about an hour in camp that morning and Ari spoke again about different kinds of shelters and other places where one could take refuge from the elements if need be. He talked about the need to work towards becoming 'just another animal' in the forest, of blending in and toughening up so that one could survive and thrive in the bush.

After we were done eating and taking down the shelter we made sure that everything was as it had been before. The idea was to leave little or no trace. Ari explained that the fire pit had been there long before he discovered the place and so out of respect it was okay to leave such things as they were.

The rest of the day was spent walking down through ravines and along the down-slopes of the mountains. We followed streams and creeks and at one point found ourselves walking along a fairly wild stretch of the nearby river.

I learned about the Fourth Shield, or the respect for and finding of water. Ari taught about the ways of finding clean water, the natural sources of water and the importance of water in the sacred balance. He also taught me a few Thornish rituals of thanks to the ones he called the Water-Folk.

'Water is very powerful. Very magical too,' he explained. 'It can be as subtle as summer morning dew or it can be as obvious as a huge waterfall. It can turn mountains into sand dunes over time and as it can give life, it can just as easily kill.'

Ari showed me a lot of things that day, so many I was starting to think I would have a difficult time remembering everything. This fellow knew so much…he was like a walking encyclopedia of wildlife and the open country.

I spent some time wondering where I would be camping that evening. I said nothing to Ari because I didn't want him thinking I was getting impatient or anything.

Eventually the trail we were on began to climb and before long we came out of the bush and onto a lonely stretch of gravel road. This quite surprised me. I had not been expecting that we were so close to civilization during our walk through the woods.

'This is more like a graded logging road,' he explained after noticing my momentary disorientation. 'Not a lot of logging up in here these days and you will find that most of the mountains around here have these roads.'

I walked out onto the brownish gravel and noticed that the feel under my feet was considerably different from the relatively soft soil of the many trails we had been on. I was starting to notice more and more subtle things as the days passed and found I actually enjoyed the contrast between the trails and the road.

'If you do see a logging rig coming down one of these roads give 'em lots of room,' Ari added. 'They are big machines and some of these roads aren't so wide.'

We walked along that road for a considerable time. I estimate that we had been out there for at least a couple of hours. Not once during our trek did we see any sign of traffic. A few times we saw deer crossing the path quickly ahead of us, and once a curious raccoon made his way from one side of the road to the other before disappearing in the bush.

Ari was silent for a good deal of our trip along the forest service road. He had been quite chatty when we were on the trails, when he had been teaching me about water, yet once we came out onto the road he became quite the opposite.

Eventually he explained that he had been contemplating the things he was teaching me. He told me I needed to realize that what he was showing me was but the tiniest fraction of what I would need to know if I wanted to walk in the ways of his tradition.

'It's like an appetizer plate at one of those fancy restaurants,' he said. 'It gives you a little sample of this thing and a little sample of that but in the end it's just a taste. That's exactly what this is. It's designed to give you a little bit of experience so you can build on this on your own.'

I understood what he was saying. I realized it would take a lot of practice and a lot of work on my own—without a safety net—before I felt competent in the woods.

'So this is why it might seem that I have only shown you this or that in a somewhat slipshod fashion. There's method to my madness and eventually you will figure out what that is. But for now I am giving you a hint of some of the deeper things you should learn.'

Suddenly, as we rounded a gentle curve in the road, Ari took a step off the road and was back in the forest. I hesitated only for a moment before I realized there was a faint trail between the boles of two birch trees.

Ari struck off along the trail and I followed him as there was no room to walk abreast on that narrow path. Eventually I could smell wood smoke but the source kept disappearing and eluding me as I walked.

'So, Carolyn,' Ari said, 'The Fifth Shield is something we will cover later on so I won't go into it in any detail here. I may not even give you any hands-on but instead cover this sacred way in theory only for now. It is a very sacred thing and I feel you need time to reflect on what I have already shown you before we go any further in that direction. The way of the Fifth Shield is the way of the hunt and it is something that needs a clear focus to teach and to learn.'

I nodded before realizing Ari couldn't see me bobbing my head from behind him. 'I understand,' I said finally.

A moment later we came out of the forest and I found myself standing in a small driveway clearing in front of a house.

'This is the home of a dear friend of mine,' Ari said. 'And I figure now is as good a time as any for you to meet him.'

9. The Sixth Shield

The house was set back against the stone of the mountainside, surrounded by various kinds of berry bushes, all now free of green leaves. It was built of a combination of red brick and wood-frame with a cedar-shingled roof. On one side there was a large lean-to shelter that could have been a carport but instead was filled with piles of neatly stacked firewood.

In front of the house was a fenced area for a fair-sized vegetable garden, now sleeping for the winter. From the peak of the roof a grey curl of fireplace smoke drifted out on the breeze.

It was not a large house but it looked quite cozy. I wondered if I was about to meet someone else who was a bit like Agnes.

Ari walked up to the door and gave a firm, loud knock. I listened for some kind of response and even though I was right behind him I heard nothing. Yet Ari obviously did, as he opened the door and walked right in.

A very powerful scent gusted out of that place and caught me off guard. I had spent days breathing in the fresh brisk air of the mountains and forest and now I was suddenly hit with a rush of spicy smells. There was wood smoke and the rich scent of herbs and spice mixed with some kind of fragrant incense, topped with another musky smell that at first I couldn't put my finger on. I was surprised when I realized that the mystery smell was marijuana. The strong scent of it wafted out the front door right along with the rest of the intriguing smells now I was even more curious to meet this friend of Ari's.

His name was Tiva and he wasn't anything like I thought he would be. For some reason I expected him to be a woman.

Tiva was not a large man but somewhere on the smaller side of medium in height and build. He looked to be somewhere in his early sixties, yet as he stood there in his kitchen smiling at us I could see a boyish charm sparkling in his eyes that suggested he might be younger than that.

He had the facial features of a white man yet with a very deep tanned-brown complexion. This was set off by a full head of Jamaican-style dreadlocks that would have come all the way down to his waist if they weren't tied back in a ponytail. The dreads were a light gray color, tending towards white, and they contrasted strongly with his skin and dark brown sweater, as did his very short, neatly trimmed goatee and white teeth. He had two gold earrings in each ear and his eyes very dark brown, seeming to be the only feature that really belonged with the color of his skin.

'C'mon in bro and young lady and don't mind da mess,' he said in an odd sounding accent that was just as difficult for my mind to place as his initial appearance. It sounded a bit Irish but also a bit like a Jamaican patois. It was very soft, rounded, and almost subtle, yet also very noticeable at the same time. I will not even attempt to write down any of his speech the way it actually sounded but it was very musical and fascinating to listen to.

Another thing that hit me right away about Ari's friend was the energy he gave off. This guy was a very powerful person. I felt like I was in the presence of some kind of a prince or a powerful nobleman for some reason even though there was nothing about his appearance or his humble little house to cause me to think that. There was a very deep feeling of power and respectability about Tiva and as he came shook my hand I almost found myself bowing in deference.

Tiva's house was even more of a witch-cottage than Agnes' place. The inside was built to last with wood paneling above a lower section of rounded river stone and bricks. A very nice arched fireplace in the center of the living room was surrounded by a trio of overstuffed, well-worn chairs, and the walls were lined with shelves containing books and all kinds of interesting little things. Ornate boxes and statues of animals and people peeked from little cubbyholes on the shelves along with an interesting assortment of crystals and colored stones.

The kitchen, directly off the living room, held a large, well-maintained wood cookstove in black and silver. Surrounding this were counters of highly polished yellow wood and a small refrigerator built into a wood cabinet. Plates and coffee mugs were visible in a number of small wooden cabinets without doors. One or two cabinets also held an assortment of mysterious-looking glass bottles of many different sizes and colors.

Bundles of drying herbs and small glass lanterns hung from the wood-beamed ceiling. A low fire crackled in the fireplace and several small candles burned in ceramic holders, filling the air with the smell of beeswax. As I stood there marveling at how cool Tiva's home was I also noticed a number of round rag-rugs woven by hand, all very colorful. Some were under the furniture and others lay on the plain, well-worn floorboards of the house, bringing a lot of color and life into the place.

It was a truly magical place and I felt honored to be invited inside. It was like Agnes' place in some ways but much smaller, much more compact and cozy. It was very different from Ari's home which, while very comfortable, was much more utilitarian, perhaps due to Ari's past as a military man.

Ari made introductions and Tiva invited us to sit down. I paused only long enough to take off my coat and boots before I complied.

I sat on the far side of the fireplace. Almost immediately I was joined by a large, white shorthaired cat who jumped purring into my lap.

Moments later Tiva came over and sat down in one of the chairs. He deposited a large, brown ceramic teapot on the well-used coffee table along with three cups. He poured and within a moment more I found myself savoring a delicious cup of mint tea.

'So, Carolyn who-has-no-tribal-name-yet,' Tiva began, 'Ari tells me that you come to my house to learn some things from me.'

I had no idea what things but I assumed Ari brought me to this place for reasons that were more than simply social. I nodded my head, to which he simply smiled and tipped his teacup towards Ari.

'This fella has always played the cards close to his chest.' He grinned.

Ari returned the grin and the salute to his friend. I could immediately see the deep and long-standing bond that they shared. They were as at ease as two brothers and I had a sneaking suspicion they were brothers by oath.

'Tiva is far more qualified to teach you about the Sixth Shield than I am, even though I know a thing or two about that,' Ari said. 'He's been a Farer for a long, long time and has a lot to pass along.'

Tiva looked at me over the edge of his cup and said, 'I bet he is teaching you the Fifth Shield last, am I right?'

Ari laughed. I nodded.

'He says that he may not even show me that one yet,' I replied.

Tiva nodded.

'He always saves what he thinks is the best for last. I will let you in on a little secret and say that what I can teach you is pretty interesting as well.'

'I will do my best to learn anything you have to teach me,' I said.

'He carries a spear and those who do that love to hunt. The hunt and the gathering of food in that way is a very religious experience for them, a holy act,' Tiva said. 'People like me carry a forked Faring stick. We gather things as well, but the things Farers go after are knowledge, lore and deep understandings. That's what we hunt.'

'Also very sacred,' Ari added. 'No less worthy than the way of the spear.'

Tiva nodded once more in a sign of acknowledgement and respect to his friend's words.

He gestured to the fireplace, where a long polished staff with two sharpened pointy tines rested against the wall. The staff was about 6 feet long and was stained a deep, almost cherry, red. It had symbols I did not recognize carved into it and inked in black. It also had several beautiful feathers tied to beaded leather thongs hanging from the base if the forks.

'We have a difference in opinion as to what Shield is the greater teaching, you see,' he smiled, 'but it's all in fun. We know that they are all equally sacred.'

'He is an elder and elders are always right.' Ari chuckled.

'You could be but you won't admit you are an elder. Just a little lad who not want to grow up and ting,' Tiva teased.

Ari just smiled and relaxed into his seat with his tea.

This time I didn't get left out in the woods. Tiva's style of teaching, just like his home, was different from Ari's. Tiva invited both Ari and me to stay with him for the next three days and said if I looked like the kind of person who was open to learning what he had to teach, he would be happy to teach me more.

Tiva had a spare room for Ari in the back part of his little house, but there was no room inside the house for me. He escorted me outside and around the back of his home to a very cute little cottage covered in leafy vines. The interior was tiny but it sported a cozy kitchen, a wood stove and a small quilt-covered bed with a wooden frame. Tiva apologized that there were no inside 'facilities' and showed me the way to a well-kept outhouse not far away.

'Student or not, a lady needs to have her space,' Tiva said as he showed me the little place. 'I hope this will do for you.'

And it did do for me, quite nicely. The tiny cabin was perfect and beautiful. I felt at home right away.

Over the next three days Tiva began teaching me about the spiritual nature of the Thornwood. He taught me some of the same basics Agnes and Ari had covered but he went into much greater detail.

What Tiva taught me about the nature of Thornish spirituality was very deep, so again I won't go into depth on these things. This is not so much a how-to book but a way of telling a bit of my own tale. I will leave the real details for those people who truly find their way to the keepers of this tradition.

However, I will outline the basics of what I was shown because I think that it is a very important part of what it means to be Thornish. Without the spiritual basis the Thornwood would not really be the mystical tradition that it is but instead simply a good set of survival tools.

I spent the first day with Tiva alone. I fell asleep in the comfortable little bed quite early on the day we arrived. I had been doing so much and trying to absorb and learn so much that I really was exhausted

I slept extraordinarily well and woke up the next day to the sound of chopping wood. When I came out of the little cottage I found Tiva nearby merrily chopping logs and tossing split wood onto a big pile. It looked like he had been at it for some time by the size of the pile yet he didn't appear tired.

He stopped chopping when he saw me and extended a kindly hand in greeting.

'My brother is gone off to do a few errands,' Tiva said after he released my hand. 'I think he figures he would only be in the way of my teachings. No doubt he will be back later.'

'Ah,' was all I could say to that.

'I think maybe breakfast might be doable, eh?' he suggested with a smile.

Pancakes, moose meat sausages and steaming cups of tea were just perfect for breakfast as far as I was concerned. Tiva was quite an accomplished cook.

'I don't eat too much meat,' he told me as he cooked. 'It takes away from the sharpness of the mind and spirit if you eat too much of it.'

He turned and looked at me quite seriously. 'If you can, never eat the meat that comes from the stores. It's a nightmare what those people do to our animal brothers and sisters, not to mention all the chemical poison that goes in. If you gotta eat meat eat only meat that has been taken respectfully with offerings by a wise hunter.'

He told me that commercially produced meat was not only bad for you but it also carried along the fear and misery inflicted by the meat farmers, and could bring ill luck on a person who was eating it.

'Luck is a very real thing,' Tiva told me. 'If you don't already know this you will soon understand what it's all about.'

While we ate he said he would like to spend the day talking about Thornish spirituality and, unlike Ari who much preferred to teach outside, Tiva suggested we spend time right where we were in his house.

We chose comfortable spots before the already crackling fire. As I carried my tea in and sat down, Tiva began to talk. He was a great storyteller and was very passionate about the things he was teaching me. As he spoke I felt myself relaxing more and more into the comfortable chair and I opened my imagination to try to visualize the things he was speaking of.

'There is so much to teach,' he said. 'I have taught quite a few people our Thornish ways yet it seems like every time a new one comes along I feel a kind of confusion. I get so excited that I want to teach everything but I know this isn't possible so I have to pick and choose what I can pass along at any given time. It is frustrating sometimes, but in a good way.'

'So are you going to be my teacher now?' I asked.

'Well, what I am doing now is showing you the basics of our ways. That way you will be better prepared and it might help you figure out what you want to study. There are basically two streams of doing things in the Thornish ways and these are, as you have probably already been told, the Faring way and the Spear way.'

'Yes, I have been told that by Agnes and by Ari, too.'

'The Farer way is the way of the spirit worker,' Tiva explained. 'The Farers are seers, oracle workers and the wise ones who work in matters of spirit and power. The Spear way is more of a Warrior way. Those who walk in this manner are often more concerned with worldly matters than those who walk the Farer way. Now don't get this wrong—all Thornish people are deeply spiritual folk. It's just that some people are more gifted in certain areas than others.'

'I understand that.'

'We are giving you these teachings now, in the beginning, so you will be able to get a feel for the path you are most drawn to.'

My mind went back to the analogy that I was standing at the tiniest tip of a very massive and deep iceberg. So much more was there, just beneath the surface, than I had originally thought. I was glad there were areas of specialization within the Thornwood. I couldn't imagine, given the amount of stuff I was now sure existed, that any one person could master it all.

'So now I will tell you a little tale as a way of introduction to these things,' Tiva said.

* * *

There was a young man who had been a very lost person for a great many years. This young man had done his share of things in the world, good and bad, and he had had his share of adventures and relationships. But eventually all of the hard living caught up with the young man and he became very sick. He thought he had developed some dreaded disease such as cancer but in the end the medical people could find nothing wrong with him.

Despite this the young man still suffered. He tried many ways of getting well. He gave up eating different kinds of foods which were bad for the health and he gave up smoking cigarettes and drinking liquor. Even after he had given these things up the feelings of illness he had did not go away.

Months passed. Years passed and the man, now no longer so young anymore, very worn out from his condition, contemplated ending his own life.

A good friend helped him out as best as he could. The friend was very caring and proved to be an ally for the now-not-so-young man. One day the friend suggested that they go on a trip together and that while on this trip the now-not-so-young man might find what he needed to heal. The friend suggested this because, as he explained to the now-not-so-young man, he believed the illness that was stealing the light from his life was not physical at all. He thought it was perhaps a sickness of the soul.

And so the two friends went off on a journey together. Their journey took them to the far-off land of Ireland, where both of them had some ancestry.

The two friends went off to explore the green land. At first the now-not-so-young man felt quite a bit better because he had become excited about the prospect of journeying through Ireland. Yet after about a week his old pains and discomforts started to creep back in again and he told his friend he was thinking of returning home early.

The friend understood but asked of him a favor. During their trip the friend had gone off on his own several times. The now-not-so-young man had assumed his friend had interests he had not wanted to bother him with. It turned out that the friend had made the acquaintance of a traditional healer and he wanted the now-not-so-young man to go and meet with her.

This did not go over so well with the now-not-so-young man. He felt he had wasted much time going to the medical doctors and getting no results or help from them whatsoever. He was also somewhat angry for he felt his friend had gone behind his back looking for medieval' help for him.

The friend explained he had found a healer, not a doctor, and the woman he spoke of was someone who was recommended to him by a family member. The friend then confessed he had been genuine about his desire to visit Ireland and go on a great adventure with his friend however, as the friend had traveled much and was very worldly wise, he also had an ulterior motive: to get his friend to what he called a 'real healer.'

Strangely the now-not-so-young man found he could not get angry with his friend for that. He realized his friend was only trying to help him heal and he probably wouldn't have come on the trip had he initially known about the healer. And so, trusting his friend, the now-not-so-young man agreed to see this healer person.

The next day his friend dropped him off. After making introductions, told the now-not-so-young man he would come back for him in an hour.

The healing person was not an old lady as the now-not-so-young man had assumed she would be. In fact, she appeared to be in her mid-thirties. She did not operate out of a clinic or anything like that. She lived in a small house off a quiet road not far from the city of Dublin. The healing woman asked him all kinds of unusual questions and, with his permission, examined him by walking in a circle around him. After she had done this she made tea for them both.

The now-not-so-young man was quite surprised by the entire experience with this strange, yet very ordinary-seeming woman. Indeed, they had a very pleasant conversation about a good many things while he sat there in the kitchen of her modest home. He felt very relaxed and comfortable and he had a gut feeling that she was genuine, both in her reputed talents and her desire to help him heal.

At last she told him she had an idea of what was wrong with him. She suspected he had become ill because he had strayed from his destined path. She told him that every once in a while there are special people who are chosen by the gods to do certain things. These people have a special fate and their threads are woven very closely with certain important things that the world needs. When a person strays from their destiny they become spiritually unbalanced and can get ill in ways that no modern medical practitioner could possibly understand. The healing woman told him she believed he was one such person and if he wanted to get well he needed to do what the gods wanted him to do.

The now-not-so-young man asked what he should do about this and she told him that he should go and spend time with his ancestors to see what they had to say. Still the man had no idea how to go about doing this. The healing woman took mercy on him and offered some guidance. She told him that he had ancestors from Jamaica and she felt they were calling him to go to that land.

He was surprised at her words since, while he had some elements of African heritage, anything that was specifically Jamaican in origin could not be seen. He wondered if his friend had mentioned this, yet he believed that not even his friend had known in detail about his ancestry. Regardless, he felt a strong determination to do what she had told him to do. He was amazed at how good the thought of traveling to that southern land made him feel.

He thanked the lady very much and asked her what her fee would be for helping him so much. She said if he had nine copper coins she would take those. The-not-so-young-man was astonished but he did as he was asked and handed over the only copper coins he had on him, which happened to be nine Canadian pennies.

* * *

'You see from my face that I have the blood of different families,' Tiva explained in that mysterious yet lovely accent of his. 'A bit of this and a bit of that, but my mother's side had some African blood. My father's side had a lot of things but the Irish were in there too. I was very surprised she knew about my Jamaican ancestors.'

'So you were the now-not-so-young man,' I said.

'Yes ma'am,' Tiva said with a smile. 'And the not-so-young-man traveled to Jamaica. When he was there he didn't find any living ancestors but a lot of dead ones. He traveled all over that land and had a number of powerful teachers. He was given a few names when he was there as well, one of them you know.'

'How long did you stay in Jamaica?' I asked.

'First time I was there for a year,' he replied. 'But my work wasn't done. I went back again for two years more but that still wasn't enough. Finally I went back there and stayed eighteen years. Finally I felt I had learned enough. I came back home and met my old friend again. It turned out that he too had been busy and he had things to teach as well. And here, years after that, you find me here in my humble home.'

'The friend you spoke about was Ari?'

'You are a smart girl.' Tiva nodded, grinning. 'But I guess if you weren't smart you would not be here, right?'

'And you got well, didn't you?'

Tiva's face went somewhat sober at the question.

'Yes, but it took awhile,' he said. 'It took a tremendous effort of spirit and of the body. I had a lot of lies floating around in my head and a lot of poison in my soul even at that point. But I learned what I was taught and I became so much more than just well.'

'But with the help of the gods you eventually healed,' I suggested.

Tiva looked at me with an even craftier grin than he had worn earlier.

'Ari will have told you something, I think, about the Thornish perception of the spirit world. If not him then Agnes will have.'

'Both of them have taught me about that to some extent.'

'To the outsider it can sometimes be difficult to grasp,' Tiva said. 'We always seek the most primal aspects of the spirit world that we can find because they are closer to the ultimate truth. The more modern something is, the more time something has had to be modified, told differently, colored by individual perceptions of the tale tellers. The more ancient things have been less…diluted.'

I understood what he was saying. It was a wise thing to look for the source of the lore that they held so close.

'We still honor them, the ones we call the Elder Kin,' Tiva continued. 'But we don't see them as omnipotent or magical folks. Their intelligence, wisdom and technology are vastly greater than our own. We see them differently, just as we also see people of the spirit world and the various nature powers differently than most. We have different names for many of them. Names that we feel describe them better, at least for our uses.'

Tiva took a long sip of his tea.

'Look back far enough and you will see the primal forms,' he added. 'They have been known to humankind for countless millennia and despite the efforts to wipe them away by misguided desert religions they live on. How could it be otherwise? We are their relations.'

I hoped he would talk more about this. I wanted to be able to put pictures in my mind of these ancient and powerful beings.

'I know about the Dark Mother,' I said. 'I have learned a lot about her from Agnes.'

'If you think you know much about her, you probably don't.' Tiva winked at me mischievously. 'She is almost impossibly ancient. Inextricably interwoven with the threads of destiny, that one is. All Thornish people have a special place in their hearts and their loyalty for her. She is the winter and springtime all in one. The beginning and the end of the trail. Men knew about her so far back they were probably little more than animals under a starry sky so ancient if we were there we could look up and not recognize the constellations.'

'That would be a long time ago,' I said.

'Then there are others,' Tiva said. 'Like Var the Far-Farer. Dark, mysterious and unknowable he is, always looking for knowledge. Hungry, ravenous for it. Very dangerous and yet an unbelievably powerful teacher. Qor is a warrior of the mountains, hard as a rock, who loves humankind and often battles those who would harm the Middle World. There are a number of these. Others are simply described, such as the Wood-man or Grandmother. In time I will teach you what I know about these folk.'

'Var sounds a lot like Odin, who Ari talks about,' I suggested.

Tiva nodded.

'Var is unbelievably ancient. When we get past all of the names and labels we see the essence of the Elder himself. The same with Qor, who some equate with Thor of the northern traditions. Who is to say that Qor of the mountain and Thor Odinsson are not the same person? Or perhaps they are not. A Thornish person seeks to remove themselves from the modern need to categorize, label, and box everything because there are far more dimensions than the ones we can perceive.'

'I think I see where you are going with this,' I said.

'I have already gone there.' He smiled. 'And returned home with a few things to teach.'

'But I have drifted off course here,' Tiva chuckled at last. 'I was wanting to speak with you about the Farers.'

'The Farer way is a spirit way,' he went on. 'Those of us who take up the staff walk the spirit roads and these roads can be every bit as much of a challenge as the road of the hunter or the fighter. We go to very dark and very scary places sometimes and we fight when we need to. Ari thinks you will probably walk the Farer's way, as Ciarán…Agnes…does. I think you might as well, but a lot of things remain to be seen. I walk the Farer way so that's what you are here to get a glimpse of.'

And with that Tiva told me more about the cosmology of the Thornwood.

I looked up suddenly and realized that while Tiva and I were sitting in his living room the entire day had passed us by. Tiva was a good teacher and in his efforts to teach me a little about the way he walked he often veered off into little side stories and anecdotes. I realized, even more so than when I was with Ari or Agnes, that the world I was stepping into was vast beyond imagining.

Not for one moment did I ever doubt a single word that came out of the old man's mouth. No matter how improbable or even downright crazy one or two of these things sounded, I knew in my heart he was speaking the truth.

Tiva taught me that while various Thornish people might embrace slightly different paths along their journey the goal was always the same— to serve the sacred balance of nature and, in doing so, seek the deepest possible understandings of the First Knowledge. As I had been taught by both Agnes and Ari, the First Knowledge was known as the Black Root among the folks of the Thornwood. It was seen as being the original understandings and instructions to humankind from the Elder Kin.

'We don't often refer to them as gods or goddesses,' Ari had explained. 'This is because in the Thornish way we see these elder beings, those who either created us or aided in our creation, as our relations far back along the line. The word Elder Kin better expresses this and reminds us of the level of respect in which we hold them.'

'So Thornish people don't know if they actually created us or not?' I asked.

Ari smiled and told me there were things that we as a culture could no longer remember. This was one of the reasons we sought the deeper, more ancient knowledge, so we could once again recover this knowing.

'The most popular theory amongst us is that the animals we now call humans were already here in the Middle World when the Elder Kin arrived. It is thought that we came from a far more ancient source, the Great Essence,' Tiva said suddenly.

I started as he said this and I wondered if the otherwise friendly old man could read thoughts.

'A more ancient source?'

'Agnes has taught you about the Dark Mother?'

'Yes,' I replied. 'She is deeply devoted to her.'

'In the way we walk, we Thornish folk, it is said that the Dark Mother is the gatekeeper, that she is the Daughter-of-the-Great-Darkness. It is believed that the Dark Mother is the mother of the Elder Kin and other ancient ones. The Great Darkness, or Great Essence, is the intelligence of the multiverse. It is the spark in the dark, so to speak, from which the sacred balance came.'

I tried to imagine a great intelligent idea out there in the middle of the darkness. It was a difficult idea to get my head around in one way and yet it all made a kind of sense to me at the same time.

'And all of us were, at one time or another, tinier sparks in that darkness,' he said. 'Each life is a little ball of light that from time to time chooses to live in a physical world. When that happens we move into a body and experience things. This is done to learn and grow. When the physical body dies the little sparks go back to the spirit world where they learn different things until it is time to go back to a physical existence again.'

Tiva paused for a moment to drink his tea.

'We are all little balls of light. We are spirit people riding around in a wagon made out of skin and bone so we can exist and learn from this world.'

'And the spirit world is darkness? That sounds kind of grim.'

'No, I said we come from darkness,' Tiva said with a smile. 'The spirit world is a matter of perspective to each individual but it is anything but dark…at least for most of us.'

I asked Tiva what role the Elder Kin may have played, if they came after human beings were already here.

'They helped us become the intelligent beings we are,' he explained. 'We were probably simple monkey creatures before they found us but they…modified us so that we could evolve in this way. It is believed that, in order to do this, they used their own essence. This is why we see them as true relations.'

I sat for a long moment in the semi-dark, pondering what he had said.

'Wow,' was the extent of my reaction, silly as that might sound.

Over the next few days Tiva and I wandered through his garden and even though it was already asleep for the winter he pointed out a great many different plants, herbs, and fungi. He was very knowledgeable in their uses. He explained to me quite frequently that what he was showing me was the merest tip of the iceberg as far as all of the understandings which Thornish people held. My visit to his house was the introduction to the Farer's way and by no means the main body of the tradition.

Finally, on the third day, as we were taking a walk through the local woods, Tiva pointed out a small patch of pretty red mushrooms with white dots all over them. They were nestled up against a tree in a way that made me think of the fairy tales I had heard as a child.

Tiva explained that these particular kinds of mushrooms were especially sacred to the Thornish traditions because they were not toxic to humans and because they granted access to the spirit world.

'Only trained Farers use them,' he said. 'They take a good amount of training to understand and can be quite dangerous to the unwise. They are very sacred and they are very intelligent in their way.'

'Do Farers always use plants or herbs to go to the spirit world?' I asked.

Tiva replied that most Thornish folk who sought visions and teachings from the spirit world did not use the sacred plant helpers for this, yet some of the Farers did use them when they felt the need.

'Do you make use of them?' I asked.

'Yes, I do, but I also use other things like meditation, drumming, and deep solitude. When a person of the Thornwood uses the plant helpers they always go in a very respectful, sacred way. The plant helpers are strong teachers. They can teach but they can also bring harm or even death. It's very wise to know what one is doing and very wise to go with reverence.'

Tiva paused and looked around for a moment. It was as though he had detected something in the environment around us, something I could not sense, and was trying to get a bead on it. After a moment he turned his attention back to me.

'These are all teachings of the thing we call the Sixth Shield. Do you know much about this? Has Agnes or Ari taught you about these things?'

I told him I had learned that the Sixth Shield was considered to be spiritual teachings and it fit in with the other five teachings.

Tiva nodded.

'So you know a bit. That's good. In Thornish lore the Six Shields are the gift of Var'yolen, who is known also as Black Coyote. Black Coyote has appeared among us twice while the Society has existed and both times he has given us powerful gifts. *Var* in the Thornish dialect means dark or unknowable and *Yolen* refers to a coyote.'

'By the way,' he added, 'There is a human named Black Coyote in our tradition as well. I think you have met him. He was called Black Coyote because he is also a trickster and a teacher, and he is a person-of-power.'

'I have a feeling I might know who that is,' I replied. 'Russell's grandfather.'

Tiva smiled. 'As I said, you seem to be a sharp one.'

Tiva looked around once again. He turned completely away from me at one point and then back towards me. He shrugged his shoulders.

'Think of the multiverse as a bunch of soap bubbles,' Tiva said, continuing his talk. 'Each bubble is a universe in itself, a reality in itself. The larger cluster of bubbles is the multiverse. Now imagine with these soap bubbles how some of them are far apart, by themselves, and others are stuck closely together. Sometimes the walls of the bubbles meld together. This is a good way of thinking about it because in our world the walls are thin in places where the bubbles nestle together. It is easier for us to cross into those areas. Others are not so easy. The plant helpers can open certain doorways where other things can't.'

'I think I understand,' I said.

'That's good,' Tiva chuckled. 'Maybe once you learn more you can teach me because even though the idea of a bunch of bubbles is a good illustration, the reality takes place on many other dimensions that humans like us can't even conceive. It's very complex and it's very good at keeping out those who are not worthy.'

'Kind of like locks on doors?'

'Yes, kind of like that.'

During the walk back to the house Tiva pointed out a large, angular rock that stuck jaggedly out of the dark soil. It was about five feet high and looked like it had been broken off the mountainside in a violent way, yet it was also covered with a fairly thick coating of deep green moss. It had obviously been there for a long time.

Tiva walked around the rock until he reached the side which was not visible from the trail. He motioned me over and pointed to that side of the stone, which did not have a lot of moss growing on it. There, right in the middle of the bare surface, was a strange-looking symbol painted in some kind of red dye or paint.

'There is a map for you to look at, my young learner,' Tiva said proudly. 'Can you answer me a question?'

I simply looked at him waiting for him to ask whatever he was going to ask. Yet after a moment I saw that simply staring at him expectantly would not be enough.

'I will try,' I said finally.

'Why was this glyph placed on this particular side of the rock? Can you tell me that?'

I thought about it for a moment. Was this a test of some kind? I started to get nervous but I pushed the test-anxiety away with a few deep belly breaths. I began to think of the four directions and wondered if it had been placed with some cardinal point on the compass in mind yet that did not seem right to me. I looked around the landscape and noted what features I could. I even looked into the tree tops above where we were standing, yet I could come up with no solid answer.

I shook my head.

'Hazard a guess, wishae?' Tiva said with a warm, grandfatherly smile. He could see my frustration building and I don't think he wanted me to suffer too much.

'Wee-shay?' I asked, pronouncing the term he had just spoken.

Tiva rubbed his chin for a moment before answering.

'You get so used to using so many words and sometimes you just accept them without bothering to think how you would explain them to someone…outside. Hmmm. Like most Thornish words it has no direct parallel in English. We take it to be a kind of endearing term. It very roughly means someone young who is learning, if you get my meaning. It is respectful, so don't worry.'

I smiled back. I was learning a lot of very interesting tidbits. I wasn't simply taking lessons in some college course. I was learning a culture from the bottom up.

'Hazard a guess?' Tiva said once again, bringing me back to the question.

'If I had to guess I would say that the painting was done on that side of the rock because there was no moss growing on that side and whoever put it there didn't want the moss to be disturbed or to grow over the mark. Also, I would say that the painting was deliberately placed so it could not be seen from the trail.'

Tiva simply beamed. He briefly placed his fingers from his left hand, palm in, to his forehead in a light touch and looked off into space for a second. He then nodded back toward me.

'Brilliant!' he exclaimed. 'You did better that I probably would have at your age, but then again I was a considerably less focused individual.'

Tiva explained the strange looking glyph. Interestingly, his mysterious accent got somewhat thicker as he spoke and he became rather emotionally charged as he taught me. This reminded me very much of Agnes when she was teaching me about the use of the world *Shar*. I was reminded again that these Thornish people were a deeply passionate bunch, and I greatly admired them for it.

'This symbol is called *Ta'Shara*,' Tiva said, gesturing towards a triangle on a squiggly line descending from inside a circle. 'In the center is the middle circle. It represents the Thornsman sitting in his place of power.

It is the goal of all Thornish folks to get to the point where, no matter what they are doing or where they are, they will always be stable, be in their place of power. Surrounding the place of power and the Thornsman is the larger circle. We call this the Deepening circle because through Deepening we learn and craft more and more powerful rituals in our lives. The Deepening is the double-edged blade because it has the power to give strength and wisdom and light, but also the power to kill.'

Tiva looked at me very intently as if to ascertain whether I was getting what he was saying. To this I nodded and this time he did not wait for me to say anything.

'The curved line descending from the break in the circle represents power and the sweep of the Thornish will. Will is extremely important and I am sure Agnes taught you about this.'

'Ari did too,' I replied. 'The Three Sisters.'

'Which three?' Tiva asked with an amused smile.

I told him of the Three Sisters that Ari had mentioned: Respect, Will, and Intent.

Tiva nodded. 'We have a saying: *Go with respect or don't go at all.* This is the basis of all ritual and indeed you will find that everything we can possibly do in the Middle World can become ritual.'

Tiva turned back to the glyph on the stone before us. 'The will of the Thornsman goes through to the blade, which is the triangle shape at the bottom. It represents the deeper meaning of Shar and the fact that whether they are initiated or not, the one who walks the Thornish ways is ever striving to serve the sacred balance.'

Tiva placed his hands on his hips and looked over at me.

'So this is Ta'Shara,' he said. 'The meaning of the symbol can go a lot deeper, but this is the basic description of it. All things in good time.'

'Ta'Shara is a Thornish word, I assume?'

'Yes,' he replied. 'It means, quite literally, 'the blade' but it is so much more than that. In the Thornish dialect we use *Ta* before something to show that it is in some way feminine. If we were to use *Na* instead this would indicate a masculine thing. In Thornish custom everything has a gender.'

'There is no neutral gender then?'

Tiva smiled again. It made me wonder if there had ever been a Mrs. Tiva and if he had any little grandchildren to beam that wonderful smile upon.

'There is *Sa*, which is sometimes used, but not often,' he said. 'For some reason we really like to have things either male or female. Oh, and since we are talking about the dialect, there is a fourth one we use and this is *Wa*. Wa indicates something that is held in high esteem, as in something sacred or highly respected.'

'Like Wataan?' I asked, recalling what I had been taught by Agnes.

'Yes indeed, though the apostrophe has been lost. But yes, wishae, you are certainly right.'

'How many of these glyphs are there?' I asked, now intrigued.

'Lots,' was all Tiva would say from behind the mischievous smile he wore so well. It was like there was a crafty ten-year-old boy back in there somewhere who refused to ever grow old.

'You have a lot to learn, young Carolyn,' he said passing by me and patting me gently on the shoulder. 'But you are coming along very nicely.'

'Thank you.' I said rather shyly. I was not the best at taking compliments.

* * *

On the evening of the third day Tiva ushered me into his tiny living room after we had eaten dinner. He brought out a small wooden bowl and a box and set them on the table. He asked me if I would like to share some sacred herb with him.

I assumed he meant marijuana. Tiva said he always referred to it as ganja and in his experience a powerful grandmotherly spirit lived within it. He spoke for a considerable amount of time on the many various kinds of ganja that were out there and told me there were two basic kinds of this sacred plant.

'Both are very sacred,' he said solemnly as he filled a small ceramic pipe he kept in the box. The small wooden bowl was half full of dried herb. 'One of the two sisters is a deep healer and a bringer of sleep and dreams. Her main job is to help animal bodies heal. The other sister is a healer more of the mind. She brings peace, happiness and introspection among other things. I am asking the second sister to join us this time.'

Tiva lit the pipe and almost immediately the room was filled with the familiar sweet, fragrant smell of the weed.

Tiva took a deep puff from the pipe and then, after he exhaled, he passed the pipe to me.

'Agnes has taught you the ways of meditation?' Tiva asked.

When I nodded he said, 'Well, in this way of taking the herb, which, by the way, Thornish people refer to as Tiva, we try to go into a light meditative state. A calm, peaceful mind will work much better with the sacred herb than a noisy mind.'

'That's where your name comes from? From the word Sativa?'

'Partly,' he confessed. 'I used to grow the sacred herb on a farm back in Jamaica. I became known for the good herb I grew and the name sort of came along.'

I took the beautiful ceramic and wooden pipe and savored the delicate aroma. Then I put the pipe to my lips and inhaled. The smoke was sweet and not overly hot from passing through the pipe stem. I took one more puff before passing it back to Tiva, who accepted it gratefully.

He took several long puffs from the pipe before offering it back to me. I was already feeling the effects of the herb so I politely declined. I realized quite quickly that this particular pipe-full was a very potent one indeed and I didn't want to get overly intoxicated by it.

Tiva respectfully bowed his head briefly over the pipe and set it down on the coffee table.

'Now relax, Carolyn,' Tiva instructed. 'Breathe deep from your stomach and count the breaths. We try to reach a calm, relaxed space to show Grandmother Tiva that we are not using her for recreational purposes.'

I did as I was instructed and in a few moments I felt a deep sense of blissful calm overcoming me. I continued to breathe and simply relaxed as much as I could.

'This grandmother is a very easygoing teacher,' Tiva said after a moment. 'And we often refer to plant healers and plant spirits as female. As you explore these things you will find that this is not simply something we arbitrarily decided on. The plant healers mostly speak with female voices. Not all but most.'

Tiva nodded from his place in the fragrant sacred smoke and smiled benevolently. It seemed to me that the natural posture of his face was to smile, unlike so many other people I had known whose natural facial expression would was either neutral or a frown.

'Grandmother Ganja or Grandma Tiva, as we call her here, really loves human beings for some reason and that's why she is so lenient when people use her in a bad way. The worst that can happen is that a person will get too much and fall asleep, but even she has her limits, so it is best to show respect always.'

'I confess I have used her recreationally,' I said suddenly, rather startling myself.

'Did you use her much for that reason?' Tiva asked.

'No, I never was one to use the herb that much. I had problems with drinking, not smoking.'

'Do you still drink?'

'Not often.'

'Good to know,' Tiva replied. 'Booze is not good in large amounts. Everything in moderation.'

And I relaxed back into the seat, drifting off with the help of the magical herb. I told the spirit of Grandmother Ganja I hoped she would show me her wisdom in helping me in my life. In response I simply felt warm, safe and loved.

Tiva was sitting across from me, relaxed deeply in his chair.

'Let's sit in the silence for awhile,' Tiva said quietly.

And we did.

* * *

Nine days had passed and once again I found myself sitting in Ari's homey kitchen with a recently emptied plate in front of me and a fresh cup of coffee steaming nearby. I had been surprised when Ari, after picking me up from Tiva's place, told me we would be heading back to his house. I expressed that surprise, saying I had expected to be out in the bush for twelve days straight.

'Life has a way of turning out different that we expect sometimes, eh?' came Ari's reply.

Leaving Tiva's house was much harder than I expected. The wily old man had a grandfatherly charm and a way about him that I found very endearing. In the short time I had been with him there was a part of me that had begun to see him as the grandfather I could never remember.

'I have no doubt you will be seeing Tiva again,' Ari said suddenly, and I felt a rush up my spine remembering what Agnes said about him. Could he really figure out what people were thinking?

'You had that wistful look on your face is all,' Ari explained. 'Russell had that exact same look after spending a few days over at Tiva's place too.'

'Ah,' I said.

Ari took a deep sip of his coffee and settled back in his chair.

'What we have been doing is giving you a little taste of things,' he said. 'Giving you an idea of what we are about and how some of the traditions work. So now you know a few things, but it's only a small bit.'

'I appreciate what you guys have taught me. It's fascinating.'

'Just the tip of the iceberg,' he replied. 'These ideas and ways, well most of them anyway, have been around for a fairly long time. We exist to serve the sacred balance in whatever way we can and in whatever way the Elder Kin might direct us to. Coming in to the traditions is a big responsibility. It's not about learning things so we can become powerful, it's more that we gain power in order to be of more use to nature.'

'I have learned a lot about that in a very short time, actually,' I said. 'Tiva showed me some things I had not expected.'

Ari smiled at that, as if he was running possible scenarios in his head. 'He certainly is an interesting fellow,' he replied.

I broached another subject I had been wondering about and which Ari himself had touched on as we sat down to coffee.

'So, can I assume we are going out again? Sort of finish off the twelve days you spoke of?'

Ari shook his head.

'Every Learner is different and we adapt what we teach – especially these early teachings – to the student and the situation. In your case I believe we have passed enough along in the days you were with me, and with Tiva. This is one of the reasons I have left out the Fifth Shield teaching for now. Later we can go into that in detail. It is very sacred and needs to be the only thing we are covering when I teach you.'

Ari paused for a moment, turning briefly to look out the window into the yard behind the house, and then back again.

'It's important that we don't expose you to too much in the beginning,' he added. 'We want to give you time to absorb it all, if you know what I'm saying?'

I nodded. Indeed I did understand. In fact, I already thought I had been exposed to too much information. I worried about forgetting some of it and I told Ari that.

'Not a problem,' he said. 'It happens and if you are unsure about anything just ask one of us and we'll be happy to go over it with you.'

Ari refreshed his coffee, pouring from the pot. He gestured that I might want a refill and I gratefully accepted.

'So if you are up for it I'd like you to hang around here for the next couple of days,' he said. 'We can putter around, get some yard work done, and you can ask any questions you like. Basically you want to let what you have been shown sink in. After that, or any time you want, we can give Agnes a call and we'll have her come and get you.'

I nodded. I would be happy to simply hang out and focus on simple things for awhile. I needed a chance to let my mind relax a bit and focus on other things. I had a lot to process, but I also wanted to simply let my hair down for awhile.

Ari got up from his seat and headed to the back door.

'I almost forgot. I need to get some meat out of the deep freeze. I think that colder weather is some of the best weather for barbecue, don't you?'

I had never really considered barbecue to be anything other than a summer thing before, but as I was definitely being opened up to new ideas and ways of doing things I figured I would go with the flow.

'Sure,' I said. 'Barbecue it is.'

10. The Deepening

I got up late one Saturday morning after a very long night sitting up reading and shuffled into Agnes' bright kitchen looking for a cup of joe. Agnes was sitting at the table reading a newspaper. She smiled up at me as I walked in.

I went to the coffee maker and poured myself a coffee, black and steamy. I looked outside at the swirling leaves and slowly let my eyes adjust to the daylight that streamed in.

As I sat down at the table Agnes got up and went back toward the area where the fridge and the stove were. She returned holding a plate with a muffin on it, a little red candle stuck in the middle of it. The candle was flickering merrily as she placed it on the table in front of me.

'What's this for?' I asked.

Agnes grinned.

'Not keeping too much track of time, are we?' she said happily.

'Well, it's not my birthday,' I said flatly. I honestly had no idea what she was referring to and I didn't have the energy to think about it too hard.

Agnes sat back in her chair with a sigh.

'It's been exactly a year since you sat out there in the hills and did your first Thornish ritual,' she said. 'A year since we started this little adventure together and I started really teaching you about our tribal ways.'

I looked at her in genuine surprise. I had indeed been aware of the passage of time, but only generally, not exactly, as Agnes apparently had been. I remembered, months and months earlier, speaking with Agnes about living arrangements because I felt as though I had overstayed my welcome. She told me I was speaking nonsense and I would be welcome as long as I wanted and she really enjoyed my company. Once I decided I wanted to learn her traditions, I went out and performed the rite that

Thornish people call a Hollowing. Her words brought back powerful memories of that day.

I stayed on as a kind of permanent house guest after that. It was not long after Agnes offered me a place to stay that I went with Russell to get the rest of my stuff from Vancouver. While I missed the beach and the life of the city I found a feeling of peace out there in the Pemberton valley that I had never known before.

So I stayed and helped around Agnes' little farm and explored the surrounding landscape when I could. I also continued to learn more than I ever imagined about the Thornish ways, not only from Agnes but also from Ari and Tiva. Despite all of that I was still quite surprised that a whole year had passed.

'I guess I might have clued in by the fact that its fall again, eh?' I said dryly.

Agnes laughed. 'Yes, well as they say, time flies when you are having fun.'

I blew out the candle with a short puff. 'Nice muffin too,' I said.

'Blueberry. One of your favorites, I think.'

'Yep. Gotta love those fresh blueberries.'

We sat in silence for a while as I enjoyed my muffin and coffee. Outside, the pitter patter of rain droplets on the window picked up. It looked as though it was going to be a cold, wet day out there.

'A year, eh?' I asked finally. 'Since you mention it I suspect there is some kind of Thornish significance to that.'

'Well, it's not specifically Thornish in nature,' Agnes replied. 'Many traditions look at the year and a day measure as being significant. In traditional witchcraft a year is considered to be a potent measure of time—especially where apprentices and other kinds of learners are concerned.'

'I see.'

'And of course this is the time, in Thornish tradition, that we who are teaching evaluate those who are learning from us and decide if they are worthy of moving forward.'

'Worthy is a pretty tough word,' I said. 'Sounds kinda unlike you, actually.'

Agnes nodded in agreement.

'It's actually the way I was taught,' she replied. 'As you probably know by now our ways aren't for the weak or the types of people who are into the flavor of the month kinds of things.'

'I know that,' I said. 'Some of the stuff you have shown me has been nothing like what I expected and some of it has been pretty tough too.'

The past year had been filled with activity, learning and working, but it had also been a time of great joy and happiness for me. In retrospect, while I had been put through some challenging teachings and had done more than my share of hard labor on the farm it never really seemed all that much like work to me. I truly felt at home in Agnes' place and I kind of felt like family in some ways. I was reminded of that old saying that tells us if we are working at something we love or in helping family, then it's not really work at all. That rang true to me, though I was still somewhat surprised that an entire year had passed while I was doing those things.

One of the things that came to mind was the day I made the decision on the Thornish path I was most interested in. One weekend in midsummer we were walking along a road by the river when we came upon a place that had been damaged, apparently by a large vehicle going off the road. By its tracks it looked as though the vehicle swerved off the road, recovered and gone on its way afterward. However, the vehicle had crashed through some bush, flattening it out and killing a number of plants and small trees.

Among the wreckage was a young holly tree. It had been broken off by the impact and thrown to one side of the path. It was an almost perfectly straight little tree, about the diameter of my wrist and about six feet long. Many of its branches had been broken leaving only a perfect two-tined fork on the upper end.

I felt so bad for this beautiful little tree, ripped out of life so violently. As I knelt to make an offering at the smashed trunk still sticking out of the ground, Agnes put her hand gently on my shoulder.

'You do well to leave an offering, Carolyn. Holly is a very sacred and magical tree.'

I did more than make an offering. In my heart I promised the spirit of that little tree that if it would permit it, I wanted to take it and make a special tool out of it. I promised I would treat it with great respect and use it to honor the sacred balance.

The tree seemed to agree and I took the shaft of wood in my hand.

'It will make a great Farer's stave,' I said.

I could see tears filling Agnes' eyes. She nodded and said nothing.

After leaving it to cure for a time, I began to work on that stick. I carved the bark off in places and left the bark on in others. I cleaned up the twin forked tines and made them into sharp points. I wrapped a length of the shaft with leather thongs and added two blue jay feathers, beaded on a red thong, around the place where the tines began. It was turning into a beautiful Farer's stang even though I knew it was still a work in progress.

I thought how I had rather wordlessly announced my intention to become a Farer. For me it was a very powerful memory and I pondered it in silence for a few moments longer.

Now Agnes' face became very sober and formal looking. I had known her long enough to know that expression preceded something very important of a traditional nature.

'And so, Carolyn,' she said, retuning my attention to the now, 'I want to tell you that I like what I see. I think you are good material for an initiation one of these days, and I want to ask you if you would like to proceed?'

'To the next level?' I asked.

'Yes,' she replied. 'To the next level.'

The next level of learning was called the level of the Seeker. I originally thought this was a kind of corny title but as Agnes explained more I realized that this level of learning was appropriately named. The Seeker was an initiated member of the tradition, not a mere Learner as I was now. Once a person was a Seeker then the true education in Thornish ways could begin. Before this point a person was being shown the very minimal basics and at the same time given space to decide if they wanted to walk in the Thornish ways. Agnes had also told me that during the first year a Learner was watched carefully to see if they had what was needed to go to the next stage of learning. It was also important for one's teacher to determine that they could actually be trusted. Trust was a big thing in the minds of the people who had been teaching me thus far. They carried their traditions with deep reverence and certainly did not want to see what they had to teach falling into the wrong sorts of hands.

I remembered well what I had been told a number of times: A person might discover the Thornish ways and decide to live in that good way, which was perfectly fine. But a person could not enter the deeper levels without initiation. *Only a Shar can forge a Shar* and a Shar is one who is initiated.

I thought about everything I had learned in the past year and about all of my wonderful experiences. I knew I wanted to learn more and I wanted to be initiated, yet I also knew from Agnes that the way of the Deepening, that ritual quest into the wild, was nothing to take lightly. I had been told that a Deepening could be a very dangerous thing on many different levels, if one did not take their lessons to heart and go with the utmost seriousness.

I thought about this in silence for a few long moments. Agnes respected my silence and gave me all the time I needed.

'Yes, Wataan,' I said, addressing Agnes as my teacher now, not simply as my friend. 'If it is something you think I am ready for, I would like to go to the next level.'

Agnes allowed herself the smallest smile.

'I do think you are ready. And since you are ready we should start preparing you for your first Deepening.'

* * *

I got out of bed early and was preparing my gear in the dining room when Agnes came in to start the coffee pot. The ground and the outbuildings were coated with a few inches of snow from the night before. It was early October and Old Man Winter had been showing his presence more and more each day. It was, as Ari said, the time of Ullr.

I had spent the previous weeks preparing as best I could for my upcoming quest. I scouted the countryside with Agnes and questioned Ari at length about the kind of place I might pick to go on this sacred journey. Both methods had borne fruit but still left me with a short list of places that might serve my purpose.

At last, with Agnes' permission, I descended into that little cellar shrine which she called the Hall of Silence. I had been in there several times before, after my initial experience with the Dark Mother. Like Agnes, I felt it was a very comforting and safe space in which to meditate. So once again I made my way in there to seek answers.

It seemed as though I was in there for hours, kneeling on the soft cushions and opening myself to anyone who might wish to guide me. I heard no voices that time, nor did I experience anything other than a picture of a clearing in the trees which I had never seen before. The picture persisted and in the end I had the impression that this might be the place I should go.

It turned out I had only been in the small chamber for about half an hour, even though it seemed like much longer. I offered my thanks and promised to leave offerings, and made my way back up to Agnes' house. There I explained what I had seen as best as I could. Agnes sat silently for a long moment trying to see if she had any idea where this clearing in the forest might be.

'And the clearing has a big stone in the middle of it. One that looks like it might have been there for a long time?' she asked. 'And you said that there is a symbol painted on that stone that looks like an eye?'

I nodded. I wasn't 100% sure that the symbol was actually painted on the rock or was the product of some natural process.

'Pretty sure, yeah,' I replied.

Agnes looked at me very seriously. 'Yeah I think I know where that is. If I don't, I bet Ari will.'

That very weekend we went out to Ari's place and he took us on a hike through the woods. The place was pretty much as I had seen it in the meditation space. It was about forty-five minutes' walk uphill from where Ari lived. I was surprised that it was so close.

Sure enough, in the clearing was a large, partially mossy stone. On one side there was a very old and faded glyph that looked a lot like a stylized human eye.

'This is a really good choice, Carolyn,' Ari said, patting me on the shoulder. 'It has been used for Deepening once before, as I recall.'

'What is the meaning of the symbol?' I asked, thinking about the Ta'Shara on the stone Tiva had shown me.

Ari smiled grimly. 'It is the eye of Var, known by some as Odin,' he said. 'A good sign to have around if you hope to gain knowledge and be open to vision.'

There was something in the clearing that I had not seen in the vision I received in the Halls-of-Silence. At the north side, tucked away among the trees, was a small lean-to style shed. It was a rectangle with a roof slanted toward the back at a 45 degree angle and made of cut pine logs, some of them no wider around than a fencepost and others about the diameter of a man's wrist. It was maybe six feet long by about four feet wide and about five feet in height. Moss covered a good portion of this tidy little box and it looked as though it had been there for a very long time.

In front of the narrow door, which was quite a small opening, there was the remains of a very small fire pit beneath the pine needles and dead leaves. It was barely the diameter of a dinner plate and edged by nine fire-blackened river stones. When I saw it I was reminded of something Russell had told me. *The white man builds a huge fire and sits way back, burning lots of fuel. The Indian builds a little fire and sits close up…and burns hardly any fuel at all.'*

'I didn't see this in my vision,' I said, pointing out the little shed. 'It looks like a woodshed.'

'I find it interesting that you saw this place in so much detail yet you didn't see the hut,' Ari replied. 'I also wonder if you thought you were going to be able to survive three nights here, at this time of the year, with just heavy clothes and a cloak? It's only going to get colder now, so you will need to be well prepared.'

'I planned on building a shelter,' I said, somewhat annoyed. His words reminded me that maybe I wasn't as smart as I thought I was, but perhaps a bit naïve.

Ari shrugged. 'Well, now you don't have to. As I say, this place has been used before in the dead of winter. That's why there is a hut here. It's not a woodshed but a hut made for the exact thing you are getting ready to do. Like I say, you chose well.'

With my destination now firmly in mind I went back to Agnes and sopped up every bit of information about Deepenings my teacher had to offer me. I had to admit, once I got over my annoyance with Ari, that he had been 100% right in giving me a hard time back there in the clearing. Even though it was not winter yet it would still get very cold and I had not been properly prepared. The thought that I had a cozy little hut to keep me warm was very comforting.

One night, as we were chatting in the living room, Agnes told me she was extremely proud of all the things I had accomplished. Choosing to walk the way of the Farer honored her even more. She gifted me with a beautiful raven feather on a long leather thong with red and black glass beads and suggested it might like to keep the blue-jay feathers on my stang company. I gratefully accepted this magical gift.

Finally, when I thought I was as ready as I would ever be, I put together a simple pack of supplies, got my head around the whole process, and prepared to go.

'Are you really sure about this, Carolyn?' she asked. 'You can always wait until spring, you know. In this part of the world it gets pretty cold and can be a harsh time to go on a Deepening.'

I told her I was ready. I had been getting a really strong vibe that I needed to do this before the winter came full on. Also, the scene I had experienced in the Hall of Silence, of a small clearing with the painted stone surrounded by snowy pines, had come to me again several times in my dreams.

'I can do this, Agnes,' I replied after a moment. 'Besides there will be less bugs…and bears.'

Agnes smiled. 'I just knew you had an ulterior motive for this. I know you don't like bears.'

'It's not that I dislike bears, but rather I am still kind of scared of them.' I grinned. 'This way they are busy sleeping peacefully in their dens and I will be peacefully freezing my ass off in the woods…in peace and uneaten.'

After breakfast we were back in Agnes' vehicle rolling down the road to Ari's place. Once we got there we piled out and went inside where Ari had hot coffee waiting.

'Enjoy it,' he said, smiling. 'It will be your last luxury for a few days.'

Agnes went out to the truck again and returned with my pack and my stang, wrapped in rough cloth. She handed over the stick and I removed the covering.

Ari was impressed with my work and told me he was not at all surprised at my choice to become a Farer.

'Somehow the two Farers you know conspired to get you on their side, didn't they?' He laughed. 'But in all seriousness, Carolyn, I think you have chosen well.'

'Tiva sent this,' Ari said, handing over a small, cylinder-shaped wooden box. I smiled, knowing full well what I would find inside. I thanked him and took the box.

'You have the things you need? Enough things to keep you warm?' Ari asked.

Agnes brought out a beautiful hooded robe of a gorgeous blue-green color. The robe had a deep hood and was made of some very heavy material. I wondered where it had come from since I had not seen her bring it with us in the truck.

She told me that she had made the robe years earlier out of heavy materials to withstand the winter winds when she went on a Deepening during the colder months. This was the robe she had done her Master's Deepening in. I was deeply honored and accepted the gift gratefully.

'It's large enough to wear a coat and even a sweater under there if you want,' she said. 'I slept in it.'

Agnes hugged me and told me again she was proud of me. With that she held the door open for me and said, 'Shall we go?'

I had been taught that it is the Thornish custom for the teacher to accompany the student on their first Deepening, at least to a point. Agnes would accompany me to the place I had chosen for my Deepening and would leave me there, returning to retrieve me once the time of the Deepening was done.

The Seeker's Deepening is typically a stationary rite and takes place in a single spot. This is done so a student has a single place in which to find solitude and not have too much on their plate. There is no hard and fast rule and if a student is deemed ready they can also consider a roaming Deepening. The roaming Deepening involves traveling from sacred place to sacred place in a kind of walking meditation and is usually practiced by Masters and Elders. They have developed the discipline not to become overly distracted by the journey or become lost, as I feared I might. It was an easy choice for me to stay in one spot.

The Deepening is not a Vision Quest in the Native sense. Agnes told me that initially people hear about the Deepening and think it is some Native ceremony but it is not. She informed me that our ancient European ancestors, and most human cultures and people, had similar ceremonies. While the Thornish folk offer great respect to the Native people of North America for their own ways, the Deepening is something that has a different flavor, as Agnes put it.

The way of the Deepening is to go out into the green spaces away from the noise and distractions of the world of men. It is a ritual in which a person tries to find a center for themselves and meditates and ponders their life, their place in the world, and tries to understand how they might be of greater use to the sacred balance. Like the Native American Vision Quest the student goes out into the solitude of nature, but unlike the Vision Quest, the Deepening does not involve fasting.

The student may take whatever food they wish though they are advised to keep consumption down to a minimum. Digestion is something that takes energy and focus away from one's body so one should eat only what they feel is necessary. Water may also be taken on a Deepening. The idea is that the Deepening is not an act of deprivation but rather a ritual where one finds comfort in their surroundings and in themselves. A person spends three nights alone in nature trying to contemplate the depths of their being and where they fit in to it all. This is why it is called a Deepening.

I should add that in the Thornish tradition there is a path of deep introspection and communication which is somewhat more like the Native Vision Quest but with a more European flavor to it. These are called *Utiséta*, or sometimes just *Séta*, by Thornish people and they often involve a 'sitting out,' usually without food or much water and often in a sacred space like a burial ground or on an ancestral mound. Thornish people are adamant about respect for local Native people and their traditions and go to great lengths to avoid any borrowing of tradition or ceremony.

Agnes walked with me to the space I had decided on. It was not a huge distance into the mountains but it had the kind of energy I was comfortable with. The area was still quite secluded and other than an old time-worn trail running near it there was no sign of civilization anywhere around.

I walked into the small clearing and set my bag down by the stone in the middle of it. I noticed that the area around the little hut had been cleared of fallen branches and the lion's share of the fallen leaves and needles. There was now a fairly new piece of canvas tarp nailed over the front entrance so that it hung down as a makeshift door flap. I had little doubt that Ari had been up here and done a little maintenance for me and I appreciated that.

'So if I might ask, what is the difference between this and when Ari had me sit out those other times?' I asked Agnes.

'Ari was teaching you different skills and understandings,' Agnes replied. 'In this case you are here because you are finding out whether Carolyn is ready to be initiated or not.'

'But you already told me I was ready,' I said, quite surprised by her answer.

'Yes, I told you that. Ari thinks you are ready as well, but at this point, before you go any further, YOU need to decide whether you are ready or not. You also have to find out from the Elder Kin and the spirit folk that have surrounded you whether you are ready to move along. That is what this is for.'

A few moments later, following a warm hug and her final instructions and encouragements, Agnes was on her way, hiking back down the trail. I stood alone in that small clearing watching her go until finally she turned a bend beneath the trees and was gone from sight.

It was still very early in the morning and the sun had not come up from behind the mountains to the east. The forest around me was very quiet and very still and on some level I felt like I was a visitor in a large library or something—encouraged by the place itself to be as quiet as possible.

I knelt down and went through my gear. I was satisfied that I had everything I needed, which was not overly much. I moved my things over to the little hut and when I brushed aside the canvas door flap I saw that someone had also placed a woven cedar mat inside over a thick layer of collected leaves and pine boughs. Again I thanked Ari in my mind. I had no doubt that he had done this.

Agnes' words came to mind as well. She told me that the Seeker's Deepening was not meant to be a hardship but rather it was a time of deep contemplation and connection with the world around me.

I spent awhile getting my gear stowed away. I hung the Deepening robe Agnes had given me on a branch nearby and then set out to gather firewood.

The first day of the Deepening was quiet. Other than gathering firewood I did very little except sit in the doorway of my little hut and listen to the sounds of the woods around me. I worked to calm my mind and become one with everything that flowed all around. I recalled the lessons I had learned, especially those given by Agnes in the Halls-of-Silence. They helped me reach a place inside that was calm and collected.

I decided not to eat that first day, other than what I had for breakfast and the coffee at Ari's. Eating was optional on the Deepening and so I chose, at least for a time, only to take water.

Time flew on that first day. Before I knew it the quality of the air changed and even before I opened my eyes I knew the sun would soon be sinking behind the mountains. I gradually roused myself from my meditative state, warmed myself by rubbing the skin of my arms through my sweater and prepared for the evening.

After that I took my offering bag with me and left offerings of sage, mugwort, tobacco and other things around the circle of my clearing. As I did this I spoke to the other ones who might be around there, whether they were in the physical realm or the spirit realm, and thanked them for letting me come to this place. When I was done I returned to my shelter space and the little fire pit.

One of the things I brought with me was a small, flat piece of granite about the size of a hardcover book, though not as thick. I picked it up during a walk along the river one day because of its unusual pinkish tinge. At first I thought it had been splashed with dye or paint of some kind but later realized it must have taken on some kind of mineral impurities that caused the tinge. Either way I liked it and adopted it as a kind of small portable altar space.

In the Thornish way there is a center of focus that is sometimes used in rituals. It involves the use of a flat stone called a *Vé* stone and a knife. The stone is called a Vé stone in reference to an old Germanic word that refers to a sacred enclosure or sacred space. Thornish people will often begin a sacred rite by placing their knife (or other item of value) on the top of this sacred stone. Traditionally this says that the person's weapons are in plain view, all is well and that a time of peace is upon the area.

This is what I did soon after I had my tiny fire kindled. I placed the Frith-knife Ari had given me edge out on the surface of the stone.

'May there always be steel upon the stones,' I said. Again this is a reference to what the Germanic people used to call Frith, which is a deep kind of understanding and peace held between people, especially in the vicinity of a sacred space. In reciting this Thornish saying I was announcing to all who were listening that I wished for peace and hale relations.

After that I simply sat there, my forked farer's stave across my lap, my knife on the stone, and worked to return to my meditations. Around me the forest turned black with night and the stars came out coldly glittering in the dark skies above.

Sometime in the middle of the night, as the cold really began to sink into my bones despite the little fire, I put on the thick robe that Agnes had given me and watched the tiny flames in front of me for a while longer. Once they died out completely I sheathed my blade with a word of thanks, doused the embers with a splash of water, and turned in for the night. I was very tired and snuggled into the warmth of the heavy robe I took little time in falling fast asleep.

When a person sits or stays in an area for a long period of time they often begin to get restless. The mind wanders and the body starts wanting to get up and go do something. This happened to me, despite my training, and about three hours after I woke up the next day I had to constantly fight the urge to get up and busy myself with something, anything, as long as it was not sitting in front of my little stone and the fire pit. I forced myself to remain where I was and focus on my breathing and state of mind. There was a battle for a while, but in the end I won out and slid into a calm, smooth awareness of all that was going on around me.

The forest where I decided to sit out was very, very quiet. I was somewhat surprised at the quiet because in the time I had lived in Pemberton and especially the time I spent in the woods near Ari's house I was always impressed with the amount of wildlife and sounds in the woods. It was not like that in the little clearing. It was very quiet, hushed almost, and I wondered if some arrangement had been made by the spirits of the place.

The second day passed much like the first and although this day seemed to take a little longer than the first one, due to the battle of wills with my body and my mind, it eventually rode down toward night. As darkness came I once again placed my Frith-knife on the little stone and said the ritual words, 'May there always be steel upon the stones.' This time, as night began to descend on the woods between the mountains, I sparked my small fire a little bit earlier than the day before.

As the flames took hold and grew brighter I took out a small steel pot, barely bigger than a coffee mug, and filled it with some water. I set this at the side of the fire so it would gradually come to a boil.

I sat there for a long while by the fire, all alone in the woods, and waited until the darkness was complete. It was like that in the forest, especially near the mountains when the sun went down. It happened quite quickly after the last rays had disappeared behind the peaks. Deep dark, like a blanket, was tossed over the land.

My little pot was boiling by that time and I reached for the tiny wooden box Tiva sent me. I knew what was inside it and as I opened the little box I felt a wave of fear go though me.

Over the past year I had seen Tiva only a few times. However, each time I visited him he introduced me to more mysteries of the Shar, and in particular, the ways of the spirit plants.

For the most part Tiva used ganja in our ritual discussions and teachings. He felt that it opened the mind to dimensions far beyond what the normally tuned mind could see and he wanted me to get to know the kinder, gentler grandmother spirit of the weed before we moved on to anything else. Tiva joked more than once that he was showing me a mere 'appetizer tray' of knowledge compared to what he might be able to teach me if I was chosen to be initiated.

Tiva also taught me about certain kinds of moss and the effects of other kinds of herbs one could either grow or find in the forest. He spoke at length about the power of mugwort and wormwood and told me much about the sacred powers found in various kinds of sage. Eventually we got to speaking about mushrooms and I could tell that Tiva held these sacred plant teachers with a very high regard.

'These relations of ours are some of the ones who are least tolerant of disrespect,' he warned me. 'You could say they are the opposite of Grandmother Ganja. They don't have time to hold people's hands. These days I think the mushroom people don't really like human beings in general. This is because of what human civilizations are doing to the Middle World, so never, ever expect a free ride from them.'

He taught me a very basic knowledge of mushrooms and said, 'Go with respect, leave offerings, look but don't touch until you are absolutely sure you know what you are doing.'

'Some of these guys will kill you very quickly,' Tiva advised. 'Others might not be so kind and leave you to a lingering, painful death. Modern medicine can't help with some of these either so be careful. Once you start down the wrong road with these folk you might be in for a very nasty end…so just don't…until you have years of study and years of earning their respect.'

I spent many hours out in the woods with Tiva and looked at books he owned, poring over many different kinds of mushrooms and fungi and the kinds of powers each of them had. A lot of what Tiva had to say about mushrooms was not found in a book but instead from his decades of experience.

Usually, at the end of the day, we would return to Tiva's comfortable little living room, start up a fire, light some candles and pass the tiny ganja pipe. He told me that in Jamaica, when people gathered with ganja for discussions, they were usually of a very sacred nature and were called Reasonings. Among the Shar these things were called Noctua and were thought of as a meeting of minds.

'A Noctua does not necessarily have to include the plant helpers in the way that Jamaican Reasonings include ganja,' he told me. 'But there are times when we do include the plant helpers at Thornish meetings of this kind.'

'The Rasta folk sound like very interesting people,' I commented.

Tiva replied that he had a lot of respect for the Rastas and the clean, balanced lives they chose to lead. He also told me that they are basically monotheists not really open to the ways of their African ancestors and that made him very sad. After that he said no more on that subject.

As the months passed I learned a lot from Tiva. I learned about Thornish spirituality and herbs and medicines as well as about the plant helpers who were sacred teachers and gateways. On the last occasion I saw Tiva it was about a month before I was ready to Deepen. It seemed to me that he knew what was about to happen because as I was leaving his house he gave me his customary hug and told me he had a feeling I might be chosen to go on a sacred journey soon—and if that happened he would be sure to send me something special.

As I looked into the little wooden box and the even smaller glass jar within I knew Tiva had kept his word. In that jar was a paste-like concoction with the consistency of butter. He had shown me this kind of thing before and used it to make tea. It was made with one of the varieties of ganja, rendered and infused with other herbal substances, until it became a kind of paste that could be eaten or added to a warm drink. I found the spirit-effect of the butter to be quite a bit different from the effect one might get if they were smoking the same variety. It was somehow much deeper and richer in texture and it tended to last much longer.

The butter I tried under Tiva's guidance was what he called 'very light and happy in nature.' I tried cookies made with it as well as tea. Both were delicious and when I complimented him on his creations he accepted the praise with a reminder that we never use the sacred ones for recreation. We always have a purpose in mind before we partake and we always go with respect.

It was at Tiva's home I learned about a variety of this sacred butter Tiva simply referred to as Blue. He showed me a small jar of this Blue once and it didn't appear blue to me at all but rather a kind of light yellow green color. Blue was a special kind of Farer's butter and it was stronger than anything I had tried previously. He told me that while it was stronger than usual, it was not dangerous but still needed to be taken with respect.

And here I was, months later in a camp in the middle of the woods, looking at the gift my friend and sometime teacher had given me. I removed the lid and took a sniff. The scent was very powerful and there was no doubt in my mind Tiva had sent along a small sample of Blue for me to use on my Deepening.

'The plant helpers are not necessary at all on a Seeker's Deepening,'

Tiva told me once. 'Most Deepenings, at any level, are done without the plant teachers. But I have long had a special feeling about you, wishae, and I think that your road might be one in which you ask for the plant teachers' help as well, just as my teacher felt the same about me all those years ago.'

I took only a very small amount of the butter on the end of my little finger and scraped it off into my cup. I took a chamomile tea bag from my pack and put that in there as well. I poured the hot water in and let the potion steep for awhile. A wonderful loamy scent rose up from the cup that reminded me of a lush forest and I knew there was no way Tiva would send along something that would harm me in any way.

After a few minutes I removed the tea bag and savored the smell of the brew steaming in the cup. I thought about my intentions and reasons for being in that place and I told Grandmother Ganja I was looking for deeper understandings about myself and my path. I was very reverent as I finally said these things aloud.

Finally I drank a mouthful of the tea. It was warm and very tasty. I wondered what else Tiva had added to the mixture because there was definitely a kind of minty citrus flavor in there behind the undeniable ganja flavors.

The warmth flowed through me and my experience at first was no different from any other time drinking a warm cup of tea on a cold night. I savored the tea and the gift my friend had seen fit to send to me.

Some time later I began to feel the tea taking effect. The world seemed somewhat distant yet I realized my senses on some levels were heightened beyond normal. I let myself drift with the feelings I was having and didn't try to resist it.

I began to focus on my reasons for coming out to the Deepening circle. I admit that I had some difficulty doing so as the tea had my mind wandering quite a bit. The effect was also a fair bit deeper and richer and stronger than anything I had experienced with Tiva before, yet I remembered his words that Grandmother Ganja would never harm me. I eventually stopped trying to direct my experience and instead let myself simply flow with it.

I had many beautiful insights during that time, some of which are, I believe, too sacred and personal for me to share here. It is said that everyone who goes to the deeper teachings of Grandmother Ganja will discover their own truths and I know for certain that this is true. Those who might read this will understand if they seek out her wisdom in their own way.

I drifted through a big part of the evening, simply flowing where the sacred grandmother wanted to take me and learning what I could. Eventually I realized I was getting tired and sleepy. I am not sure if this was one of the effects of the ganja or if my body needed rest after a long day. In any case I began to entertain the idea of offering thanks, putting out my fire and curling into my shelter for the night.

This was when the hairs on the back of my neck went straight up and a cold wash of fear spread through my body from head to toe. It seemed to me that the already chilly temperatures around me had dropped even lower.

I had the distinct feeling that something was watching me.

I looked quickly around the clearing, trying with difficulty to see what might be out there in the dark spying on me. I could see nothing and was rather surprised my small fire wasn't putting some light out there.

I realized my tiny fire was out. It was completely dark in the little pit, as though it had gone out hours ago and I did not notice. I was amazed and for long moments forgot about the feeling of being watched and instead peered at the darkened fire-pit.

The eerie feeling of being watched returned. I finally summoned my courage, took up my Farer's stave and got to my feet. As I looked up above the treetops I could see a tinge of orange-red to the peaks in the east and knew that dawn would be coming to the land soon. It didn't help me at the time because my eyes were still unable to penetrate very far beyond the big mossy stone in the center of the clearing.

The old painted symbol on the rock Ari had called the eye of Var seemed to be glowing with a mysterious light. At first I was shocked but that didn't last long. I had learned enough and experienced enough over the past year to understand that the world was a much bigger and more magical place than most human beings believed and that many things were possible that some might deem impossible.

After a long moment or two I realized that the symbol seemed to glow more when I looked at it from the peripheral vision at the side of my eye than when I looked straight at it. It was a strange blue-gold color and as I looked at it the sense of fear I had earlier was gone. I felt quiet and at peace. It was a very strange transition.

Sudden movement caused me to jump back against the small hut. A huge black raven landed right on top of the stone. The pre-dawn light was beginning to edge closer to cresting the ridge above and in that faint light I got a really good look at the bird. He was huge, bigger than any raven I had seen before, with beautiful glossy feathers, bright dark eyes and a wicked-looking black beak.

I watched him for a moment and knew that he was watching me. I realized he was looking at the feathers which hung from my Farer's stave. A feeling of warmth and understanding washed over me and I began to think maybe this wasn't any ordinary raven but the grandfather of all of them himself, *the* Raven.

I took a breath and bowed slightly before him. 'Hello, brother. How is your wife, Amber Eyes?' I asked.

The huge raven looked at me quietly for a moment or two more before nodding his big head up and down and uttering a loud squawk that echoed all through that place. With that he leapt off of the rock and took off skyward, flapping away into the west on those great big wings of his.

I sat back down, now truly exhausted, and placed my stave across my lap once again. My head was clearing and I could tell that for some time the ganja butter had been wearing off. I began to be more aware of the chill in the air and I clutched the robe around me for warmth. The symbol on the stone stopped glowing, returned to a dim figure on the side of the rock.

As I sat there in the slowly increasing light I noticed something else just as I was on the absolute edge of crawling into the hut to sleep. It was a single large glossy raven feather.

A very sacred gift from a very sacred friend.

I slept like a stone in that little hut for what seemed like way too long. I dreamed all that time of ravens and flying with ravens over treetops and valleys.

When I finally woke up the sun was nearly full overhead. I had slept until noon! For a moment I just sat there, absorbing the sunlight that warmed the forest floor. I wondered if this is what a turtle sunning herself on a rock felt like.

Then I remembered the experiences of the night before. They were powerful and vivid and I cursed inwardly that I had not brought along a notebook to write about them. I remembered the gift of the feather and for a second I panicked, thinking that the gift had only been in dream-form and not available to me in this material realm at all.

But this was not the case. There, lying next to me on the woven cedar mat, was a huge black raven feather.

The final day of the Deepening brought new insights and I returned to meditation as best I could despite the intrusion of occasional bouts of excitement over what I had experienced. I decided to dedicate the rest of the third day to an attitude of extreme thanks and humility for all the many gifts which had been given to me. I bowed my head and allowed the tears to flow as I immersed myself in the joy of simply…being.

The dawn of the following day brought Agnes back to the clearing to retrieve her wayward Learner.

In Thornish tradition many rites and ceremonies are performed at dusk or dawn. These are referred to as the times-between-times and are said to be much closer to the gateways between the worlds than other times, so I was not surprised when Agnes showed up. I was ready for her and was in the process of putting things away in my bag when she arrived.

Agnes greeted me with a warm hug and a smile and helped me pack the rest of my things. We both thanked the spirits of that place and even the little hut for the hale experiences I had encountered there. I scattered the rest of my offerings about the clearing and left several copper coins at the bases of various trees in case the Earth-folk that some call Dwarves might like to have them.

While I was leaving the offerings of pennies I noticed, near the brush at the very edge of the clearing, a perfect piece of cut birch. This piece of wood was about a foot long and about the diameter of my wrist. It looked as though it had been cut with an axe, though not recently. I wondered at that since there were no birch trees anywhere in sight and then a slight chill ran up my spine. I took the piece of birch from its little nesting place near the roots of a pine and showed it to Agnes. I was both elated and feeling like an idiot since it was only now, when I saw this perfect little log, that I remembered something very important.

Before I set out to perform my Deepening Agnes sat down with me and told me some things about the process and about the initiation I would be entitled to if I completed the Deepening. Part of the initiation process included the acquisition of a piece of sacred wood. I was supposed to look for a piece of wood that would be suitable for adding to the tribal fire during my initiation and most of the time people found that special piece of wood during their Deepening ritual.

For the first couple of days after that discussion I kept my eyes peeled for just such a nifty little piece of wood, but I wanted the offering to be something I picked up during the Deepening ritual. Once I was actually on the Deepening I completely forgot about it. It was lost in the clutter of my brain, along with so many other things I was trying to keep track of.

For a second I bowed my head toward the direction where I had found the little piece of wood. I gave silent thanks for this gift and for the reminder that it was something I was supposed to get.

'That is a very nice piece of birch,' Agnes said. 'Interesting find considering I don't see any birch around here.'

I agreed, yet I was very happy to find it. I placed it reverently in my bag and hoisted it to my shoulder.

'Thank you for the use of your robe as well, Agnes,' I told my teacher. 'Without it I would have been pretty chilly.'

Agnes smiled. 'It's yours now. A gift. You keep it and maybe one day you might pass it along to a student.'

Now there was a thought. Me, a teacher? Before that moment I had never thought of anything other than getting to the point where I felt I had learned the basics. But now that I was well on the way to initiation the possibility of actually having something to one day pass along was somewhat overwhelming.

Eventually we left, but I felt this incredible urge not to go. I wanted to simply stay there in that place and continue to have amazing and deep experiences.

'We never want to over stay our welcome,' Agnes told me softly, as always understanding where I was coming from. 'If you want we can come back to visit from time to time. Maybe after the place has recharged a little bit.'

And so we made our way back down the trail.

I wanted to spill my guts to Agnes about all of the things I had seen, heard and experienced there in that sacred bubble of time and space. However, she would have none of that. She told me that while she was very proud of me she had to force herself away from curiosity over my experiences because tradition demanded that she do so. In the Thornish way a Deepening, even a relatively lightweight one such as the Seeker's Deepening, is a highly sacred experience that can unleash very powerful things in the heart, mind, and spirit of the person undertaking it. For this reason it is considered wise for the student to refrain from talking about the experience until they have a few extra days to ponder and absorb everything. By then the person would be able to more clearly decide what things to share and what to keep private. It was a struggle, but I agreed that the tradition was a good one.

I was rather surprised that there was no sign of Ari when we emerged from the woods on the road near his house. I kind of expected him to be out in front of his house as usual with a cup of coffee in his hand.

Ari's house was uncharacteristically dark, as if he had packed up and gone somewhere. We piled into Agnes' parked truck and within moments were on our way back home.

Home. What a thought. In all my years and in all the places I had wandered I never really felt at home anywhere. Now, at last, I did and the sudden realization of this brought silent tears to my eyes. The love I felt for this land and for these amazing people was almost overpowering. They were my family on a level I had never realized would be possible before. They accepted me into their homes and hearts and really, asked nothing of me in return. The wave of love and comfort rose higher and higher and all of the things I experienced in the Deepening joined in with them. Finally I could hold it back no longer though I tried to choke back the sobs as they came flowing out.

Agnes looked at me briefly and then, smiling that warm sisterly smile, turned her attention back to the road. Even in the brief moment she focused her eyes on me I knew she gleaned the reason for my current state. I can only imagine it was because she herself experienced something similar, long ago.

'Welcome home,' she said.

11. The Crossing

I emerged from the Hall-of-Silence feeling rather groggy. The meditation had been a deep one and I got so lost in it and the warm, beeswax-scented comfort of that sacred little place I almost fell asleep.

Finally I roused myself and made my way back up to the surface level. I had been contemplating my upcoming initiation. Agnes suggested this process was like a larger version of the Hollowing. I was expected to take a good, hard look at myself and what I had learned, what I had done and where my place was in the world. I was to ponder the ways I might be of use to the sacred balance and to a larger gathering of people who would become tribal relations to me. It was daunting even though I had already performed the Hollowing ritual and had now been on the Deepening. I had learned things on both of those other rituals and I realized that there was so much more I had yet to understand about myself, my place and the things I was capable of.

I spent time in the privacy of my room thinking about many things and later wandering in silent contemplation about Agnes's property. Finally I went down into the sacred room in the sub-basement to meditate.

'Sometimes we learn the hard route, by direct experience or other worldly forms of learning,' Agnes once said. 'At other times we take the softer road to the realm of understanding and that comes through meditation, self-analysis, and introspection.'

It was with those things in mind, on that somewhat softer road, that I spent the three days following my Deepening. Agnes suggested I try to stay as quiet and inwardly focused as I could and I took her advice. Agnes was very good to me during that time as she kept to herself and out of my way, except for providing some extra-sumptuous meals.

On the third day, after I came up from the cellar, I joined Agnes in the dining room for a cup of coffee. It was a particularly bright day with the sun shining down from a crystal clear sky. Agnes' many-windowed dining area was more like a greenhouse and on days like this it was particularly bright, cheery and warm.

I had not taken anything with caffeine in it since I returned. For some reason my body was not into that kind of thing and for a time I had only water to drink. By the time I found myself once again in that sunny dining room I was ready for a warm cup of joe.

It was then that Agnes told me about the upcoming initiation. I knew before I went on my most recent ritual that by custom the Seeker's initiation usually was held quite soon after the completion of the Deepening. When I returned I did not ask Agnes for any more information. I trusted that when Agnes was ready to tell me she would— and now she had.

It had been decided that my initiation would be in two days' time and Agnes would take me to the place where it would be performed. For some reason I started to feel a bit scared and I had no idea why. I mean, I had gotten to know these great people very well over the past year and I knew I had no reason to fear them. During the past year I also learned much about the Thornish way and performed several of the rituals, yet here I was somewhat fearful of what might happen during the initiation.

It came as no surprise to me at this stage that Agnes knew exactly what I was feeling. She told me it was perfectly normal to have feelings of anticipation and even uneasiness when going into something like this. She told me that this was a very powerful transition point in my life and I probably feared that the old part of myself, which was mundane, common, and relatively disconnected to the multiverse, was about to ritually die off. This was so that the new me, the connected me, the me who was integrating more and more every day on many levels, could start blossoming.

What she said made a lot of sense and it calmed me down considerably. 'The mundane in us all is a rather insidious thing, really,' Agnes said. 'It is generally fat and lazy. It has been programmed to be a good little sheepling beast, a tame little herd animal who does as it is told by the system. It consumes and seeks pleasure but most of all obeys its world-killer masters. So this part of us wants to hang on, wants to continue to guide us all back to a dull existence that is wasteful at best and destructive at worst. On one level or another it knows you have been walking away from the program, Carolyn. It knows that its extinction is coming and that with every step you take into the Thornwood you are closer to cutting ties with it forever.'

Agnes leaned across the table in a very conspiratorial manner and said, 'Sheep can't venture into the Thornwood my friend...not unless it's as food for wolves.'

* * *

Finally the day came. Agnes told me that the initiation would happen at sunset and we should be where we were going before that time. She informed me that I should enjoy the day, which was another clear one, and I should try to find peace with my mundane self, so I would have less drama and trauma as I ritually cut ties with it.

I agreed with that and, much like the days following my Deepening, I spent the day enjoying the silence and good energy that was found everywhere on Agnes' farm.

Dinner was very light. We ate a bowl of fresh green salad with roast chicken strips on top along with a pot of delightful herbal tea. Agnes told me she didn't think it was a great idea to eat too much before an initiation, though she wouldn't say anything more on that subject.

'As I have told you before, wishae,' Agnes said, 'the initiation of the Seeker is both simple and powerful. I have prepared you as well as I can and I know you are worthy of crossing that line and really joining us. So don't worry about it and simply go with it. You will do fine.'

During the afternoon I experienced a very strong urge to paint my face in a tribal fashion. When I told Agnes she smiled and said she had done the exact same thing. So now I had a dark diagonal black stripe running from the back of my jaw just below my ear, across my cheeks and over the bridge of my nose. The black stripes were quite thick and they darkened my face considerably. I pondered braiding my hair, which was quite long, but in the end I decided against that and simply brushed it out. At Agnes' suggestion I braided some of my hair on one side and added the raven feather she had given me near the bottom. The final result was quite primal-looking and I reminded myself, as I looked in the mirror, how much the lost girl from Ontario had changed in such a relatively short time.

Agnes told me I looked like a Celtic queen from the old country. The comment took me by surprise. Must have been the wild look my red hair had when it was all brushed out and wavy. Still, it was nice of her to say.

About an hour later we were on our way. I remember thinking it would probably not be the best thing in the world if we were forced to a traffic stop or something like that. I really didn't want to have to explain to some cop why I was made up like a barbarian, though for a second the thought of it brought an amused smile to my face.

At last we arrived at our destination. It was a small meadow at the end of a side road I had never been on before. I could see no one around except Agnes and I wondered for a moment if Agnes was going to initiate me by herself.

We got out of the truck and I tossed my jacket in the truck, replacing it with the heavy hooded cloak Agnes had gifted me. I grabbed my Frith-knife from my pack and strapped it on with a nice leather belt, also a gift from Agnes. After that I took my Farer's stave and the white birch log I found at the Deepening place. I took a look at myself in the side view mirror of the truck and realized that Agnes was right. I looked like a woman out of time.

'It's time to go, wishae,' Agnes said, using the Thornish term for learner. 'Remember all you need to do is answer the ritual questions. There is no need to freak out or anything. It's quite simple.'

'I don't get it though,' I said. 'Aren't there supposed to be others here as well?'

Agnes grinned. 'We are not going to do this in full view, you know. Even though it's almost nighttime there are herd animals about —both the four-legged and the two-legged kind. It's the two-legged kind in particular that we have no wish to see interfering in our culture.'

'I understand,' I said. 'Kinda.'

Agnes smiled. 'You know what I mean. Some things are open to the world and other things are closed to the common person. Now what you need to do is to walk across this meadow, right to the end, and go into the woods where the lantern is.'

She paused. 'Remember what we talked about that one time a long while back? Where I described the Thornwood to you as if it was a forest?' she asked suddenly.

I did remember that. She had described it as an analogy; the Thornwood was a forest of thorn-trees growing in concentric circles and there was only one path to get from the outer ring to the inner core. That way was the initiatory path in which one learned from a teacher, applied what they learned and then eventually was given an initiation to the next level of learning and responsibility.

'Yes, I remember that,' I replied.

'And what is on the outside? The area outside the outer circle of the Thornwood?' she asked.

'The outer realm,' I answered. 'The place where those who are not of the tribe live.'

Agnes nodded her head. 'And what's the next ring inward?'

'Inside the outer wall is the realm of the Thornish folk,' I said. It was more complex than that but I thought it was what she was hoping to hear.

Agnes looked at me and then gestured to the forest on the other side of the meadow.

'This is an analogy in the material world to that diagram we talked about. Out here, no matter how much we have shared, no matter how much you have learned and especially, how much I have come to love you, Carolyn; out here we are still outside the hedge-wall. More exactly, *you* are still outside the hedge-wall. Beyond that meadow is a line that you will cross tonight and when you do you will be inside that first ring of thorn trees. You will really truly be one of us.'

'I get you.'

'I know you do,' she said softly.

I looked across the meadow again and sure enough I saw a tiny, flickering light in the distance. How I had not noticed it before was a mystery, but then again, Agnes had been expecting such a thing and was probably looking for it.

'Right there by the lantern is a trail. Follow it and other lights you see and you will get to where you need to go.'

I looked back across the meadow toward that tiny light at the edge of the dark woods. The sun had only recently passed beyond the mountains to the west and though true sunset was a time away the valley was already getting dark.

I looked back at Agnes. She had her backpack slung over one shoulder and her other robe, a very nice dark green one, draped over her arm.

'Now is the time, Carolyn. You have earned this. Not too many other people can say the same.'

I looked back toward the meadow again.

'I know,' I said. 'It's just that this seems to have come up so fast. I never thought…'

I turned to look at Agnes again and she had disappeared. There was no sign of her. How she had managed to walk away from the truck so quickly and silently was really beyond me. But the fact was that she was gone. I had no choice but to either stay with the truck or get going across the field ahead of me.

So off I went.

As I walked slowly across the small meadow, stave in hand, I marveled at the serenity and pureness of the place I was in. It was cold; winter had made serious inroads into the land and it was rapidly going to sleep for the season. The tall grass in the meadow was long dead and turned a wonderful golden yellow color and as I walked through it the dry seed heads brushed against my hands. A light but chilly breeze blew through the area and reminded me that there were other ways of being zapped to alertness besides coffee.

The stars had begun to come out, very faintly now, as the sky gradually turned to purple and then black. By the time I reached the other side of the meadow I was grateful for the little candle lantern with its worn metal and glass case that dangled from a tree branch.

I looked down and saw that indeed there was a trail leading off into the woods. I could see it winding a little way ahead of me but as the night deepened the woods along it became blacker, so I checked the little birch log tucked under my arm and, with my stave, began picking my way into the dark woods.

A little way along, past the first curve, I found another lantern, this one with a somewhat larger candle, more brightly lighting the way. Beyond that I saw another and another and I could tell that the trail had turned into a straighter path.

I passed three more lanterns before the path began to wind again, but I found more lanterns waiting to guide the way.

I was starting to wonder how long this trail would continue along through the blackness. And black it was—I could barely see my hand in front of my own face and the thick branches of trees overhead blocked out the sky above quite well. I felt more like I was walking down a tunnel than making my way along a forest trail. I was very, very glad that there were lanterns in there, otherwise I would have been truly lost.

At one point, at a little place along the way and around a gentle curve in the trail, where the lantern behind me was no longer visible and the light of the one further ahead was partially blocked by the trees, I stopped for a moment. Somewhere off in the dark to my right I could hear the magical sounds of a small stream singing its bright song over stones in the black. I remembered something Agnes had said to me very early on in our relationship.

'The darkness is where everything, and I mean everything, has its beginning. It is the primal place, the place of the Great Essence, the

Dark Mother and everything we hold sacred. Do yourself a kindness and spend time in the dark, Carolyn. Just listen and feel and before long you will be amazed at the things the dark can teach.'

So for a minute or two I just stood there in that nearly complete blackness listening to the little stream. I opened myself up to the experience as completely as I was capable of doing at the time and found that even with a tiny amount of effort I could sense many things I had not sensed moments earlier when I had been walking and thinking. I could feel the essences of the trees that grew close by and I could smell the many earthy smells that surrounded me. There was pine and birch and a bit of cedar. I could also feel the coolness of the earth beneath me and could smell the loamy, mossy dampness that was still there despite the cold.

I felt no fear as I stood there alone in the dark. I discovered it was becoming easier to discard the nattering of fearful thoughts and I realized most people allow fear a much larger place in their life than it ought to have. I was out in that blackness walking my own Wyrd, my own line of fate. Whatever could possibly happen to me here, in this dark place, could just as easily happen to me on a bright, sunny day. We have some say in our fates but not all and the larger threads of Wyrd are set. What use is there in feeling scared of the dark when there are many more things that may actually warrant the natural use of fear?

'The dark is deeply sacred,' Tiva had told me. 'So is the wonder of the light, but they are in balance. Anyone who focuses only on the light or only on the dark is out of balance. It's best to learn from both and be embraced by both.'

I stood there for some time. I cannot really say how long, but after a time I thanked the trees and the sacred earth and the little stream which I would never see, and I began to walk once again.

At last I could see a dim light up ahead that seemed to be caused by something other than a lantern. The light was brighter and I was pretty certain there was another clearing ahead, and in that clearing I would find a campfire.

When I came to the last lantern I was standing at the edge of a much larger clearing. This clearing was quite mossy and had short grass growing in it, and sure enough, down near the end of the clearing there was a large bonfire burning.

Directly in front of me, about five feet away, was a very powerful thing. It was a deer skull, antlers and all, mounted on a wooden pole stuck into the ground. The skull was tied onto the pole at about face height and was painted in red and black spirals, decorated with beaded leather thongs tied with various kinds of bird feathers. It looked very Celtic yet also Native in some ways.

I knew I was in the place I was supposed to be for the initiation.

It was about this time I heard the sound of drumming. I could not place where it was coming from but I assumed it was coming from the other end of the clearing.

Two very primal-looking tribal masks were tied to the trees that marked the end of the trail, one on either side of the entrance to the clearing. They were not particularly scary-looking but I had not noticed them there at first and when I finally did it was an abrupt surprise.

I looked at the masks for a moment in that still dim flickering light. One was an antlered effigy of some sort and the other one reminded me of carvings of the Green Man. Both masks looked like they were made of wood with bone and feather attached and were quite beautiful in a very primal way.

My attention was brought back to the bonfire as I made out the silhouette of a human form moving across it from one side to another. The drumming continued, low and heavy. Other than that one bit of movement I saw no indication that anyone was over there. I summoned my courage and started to walk across the clearing towards the bonfire.

A person in a hooded cloak appeared beside me. I was about halfway between the trail exit and the bonfire when the person appeared and I just about jumped out of my skin.

It was Agnes. Again I was astonished at how stealthily she could move. In all the time I had been around her I had not seen her do this kind of thing. She looked at me from beneath the edge of her robe's hood and I saw she had also brought her Farer's stave, or stang as she called it, with her.

'Glad you made it through the trail alright,' she said with just the slightest hint of humor in her voice. 'We keep going until we get to the fire.'

'I didn't realize you would be going with me like this,' I said.

'I am your teacher,' she said. 'In this tradition it is usually the teacher who sponsors the student at initiation. We know them the best.'

I nodded. She had mentioned something about a sponsor before but I guess I had not been paying as much attention as I should have been.

'Wataan,' I finally said, as formally as I could, and bowed that little slight head-nod bow I had been taught.

Agnes returned the bow politely. 'Soon you will have a new name,' she said. 'I am very excited for you, wishae.'

I walked with her towards the blaze, which by now was giving off quite a bright light. I could smell the scent of various burning herbs and incenses off to the sides and the sound of the drumming was louder and louder. The entire scene was very primordial. It made me feel as though I had been swept away in time and deposited somewhere else, thousands of years ago.

I was entranced. The primalness of the scene called to me in a very powerful way. Had this not been an important ceremony I might have given in to the sudden urge to dance wildly about that big fire.

In the brighter light I noticed there were several poles set in the earth, like fence posts only taller. These were spaced roughly around the circumference of the clearing. Each one had a primal-looking mask with various adornments like feathers, beads and bells hanging down. I could feel the presence of other people now but other than Agnes, who was right next to me, I could see no other physical sign that they were there.

'We should stop here,' Agnes said.

And so we stopped.

My eyes adjusted and finally I realized there were several people directly across the fire from where Agnes and I stood. Over the past few moments the bonfire had burned down a bit and no one had added any more fuel to it, so the flames were no longer burning as high as they had been.

As I peered across the fire I could make out three people. The one in the middle was Ari and he simply stood there in his dark-colored clothing and buckskin jacket, holding a great black spear. The people on either side of him I couldn't identify because they were both wearing tribal masks. Other than the masks they were dressed much like Ari was, in casual dark-colored clothing. One of them carried a Farer's stave and the other, like Ari, carried a spear.

Over to one side I could make out the drummer now, standing near the trees. It was my friend Tiva, drumming away happily. Tiva was dressed much as he always did although he now had a great many talismans and other ceremonial jewelry hanging around his neck. I detected the sweet, earthy scent of ganja and as soon as I spotted Tiva I had little doubt as to where the sacred smell originated.

Next to Tiva was another man I recognized and I realized it was Russell's grandfather. I felt a familiar warmth when I saw Oliver standing there. I had not seen him in some time and I missed his gentle yet humorous ways of wisdom.

I also saw Russell over there, clad in a hooded long coat and wearing a stripe of red paint across his cheeks. He was smiling, as he usually did, and seeing my friend, who felt much more like an old, old friend than a relatively new one made me feel much less anxious.

Two other people were there as well but these folks I did not recognize. In particular, there was a grim-looking man who looked like he might be a very serious fellow. He had short blackish-gray brush-cut hair and looked to be in his forties or so. He had the look of a hardened warrior about him. Like Ari he was dressed in dark clothing, wearing a turtleneck sweater under a beaded leather jacket. He held an implement in his hand that could only be one thing—the traditional Thornish weapon that shared the name with those humans who had been initiated.

'Oh, a Shar,' I said, before realizing I had was thinking out loud. I had not meant for that to come out.

'That's Martin,' Agnes said. 'You haven't met him yet. Sometimes he goes by Matt as well. He has been Thornish for a long time. His Thornish name is Shale, Master Shale.'

I had heard Martin's name before, from Agnes and from Tiva. Martin was one of only a few people who had gone all the way to the very core of the Thornwood as far as his devotion to the old ways and the sacred balance went. He was a *Vardyr*, one of the elite warrior priests—if a person could apply such a term to a Thornish person—of Thornish culture. Not even Ari or Tiva had gone that far and sworn the kinds of oaths that this Master Shale had. I was somewhat in awe of Ari and I was fascinated by Tiva but this fellow was something even beyond them. I hoped I would get to meet him.

Martin must have sensed me staring at him and, as if in answer to my thoughts, he looked over at me and nodded his head in polite greeting. His Shar, a short-hafted spear with a small, silver balancing ball on one end and a wide, wickedly sharp spearhead on the other end, glittered in the firelight.

I nodded back as best I could, feeling suddenly very small beneath the gaze of this Thornish warrior.

Ari stepped forward a pace and looked at Agnes and I across the flames from him. He raised his hand and the drumming stopped. Everything but the crackle of the fire and the light whisper of the wind was quiet and for a long minute or two no one said or did anything.

I could feel the precipice before me, opening up like a crack in the ground, threatening to swallow me up…yet in the physical world there was no actual crevice in the earth, only the feeling that I was about to irrevocably fall between one world and the next.

I felt a sudden rush of energy that almost brought me to my knees. I staggered for a second but kept my balance. I felt Agnes stir next to me but she didn't try to help. I was on my own and I knew it. This was not something that had come from outside of myself but rather a deep and potent well of emotions and spiritual energy that came from the core of my own being. I realized, in that moment, that what was happening to me was the end result not only of my training here in the valley but also of my life's journey. I had set out looking for a home, guided only by the words of a kindly and mysterious old woman. I had many adventures, not all of them good ones, but in the end, they brought me here to this place and time. I could see that everything I had done and everything that had happened to me had been simple road signs on the highway of life that led me here to this little bit of now.

I looked at Agnes out of the corner of my eye and could see the bright sparkle of her eyes as she looked out over the flames. I had little doubt that this moment was bringing back memories for her as well as stirring up the primal feelings that I was feeling in this place.

Finally, Ari raised his spear in the air.

'Let this ceremony begin,' he said.

Final Words

I hope the reader will forgive me for not going into detail about the Seeker's initiation ceremony. I have included all I could without violating the sacredness of the ceremony. Initiations, in the Thornish tradition and probably in many other traditions as well, are considered not only to be sacred things but also very private. They need to be closely kept by those people who use them and it is said that the power stays where the secrets are kept.

The Thornish way, at least the way it is practiced at the first Crossing (initiation) and beyond is an exclusive way. Only those who are invited past the veil are allowed to know the deeper mysteries and follow the path to higher levels of training. In this way the tradition not only maintains its ways in an unaltered, undiluted fashion but also exercises control over who is and is not permitted to walk in its ways. A person who is accepted and trained by an initiate may become a full tribal member and they are entitled to a tribal name. They are also entitled to be referred to as Shar or Shaara, depending on their gender.

All of these things are very special to Thornish people and they wish to see that they remain special. There are secrets and lines which I, in writing this, cannot violate.

Long before I ever wrote anything down concerning the Thornish people I asked for permission to do so. I asked Agnes at first and later Ari and Tiva what they thought about this. In later times I spoke to other Thornish people I met. I was thinking, even back then, that one day I might want to write a book about my experiences and when I asked for permission I explained this to them.

All three of the original people I asked, as well as later ones, told me that they had no objection to me writing anything down. That was, as Ari told me, my own business.

Ari, in fact, encouraged me to write about the basics of the things I had seen and would experience. He was always in support of the idea of sharing the Thornish ways with others on the outside who wished to learn.

He told me that, long ago, he had seen the time coming when more and more people would have access to information than they ever had before. He said that in this coming time more and more people would start waking up and realizing the sad state our world was in and they would begin to awaken spiritually and intellectually as a way of rising up and combating the twisted ones who currently rule our planet.

He also told me he thought the traditional way of finding out about the Thornwood—which was basically by word of mouth passed along in smallish circles—was not going to be up to the task in the future when the need for awakened warrior tribal people would be increasing. He wanted more people to know we existed and still do exist, and he wanted people to take an interest and perhaps help us to grow our numbers.

However, I was also told that if I was ever chosen to go beyond the basic Thornish understandings and training I would have to take an oath and that oath included keeping the inner teachings, the way of the Shar specifically, as a closely held secret.

So this was the idea behind this book—to give the reader an idea of what the Thornish ways are like and to describe a small portion of the amazing world this tradition walks in. It was always my intention to give people a glimpse of this hidden world and to give them enough information so if some were interested they might seek out those who know more.

It was never intended that I should break my word and insult or endanger the tribal tradition which I have become a part of. I earnestly hope that you who are reading this will understand this and know that honor and respect are very much involved here.

And so it was that I did indeed go beyond the basic training of the Thornish culture. I was initiated that night and became part of the inner tribal circle. I received my tribal name, which of course the reader will know from the beginning of this book.

In the years that followed I learned a lot more than I ever thought possible about the tribal way I had taken as my own. Once I was initiated I continued to study under the watchful eye of Agnes, who became even closer to me in ways that I will not go into here. At Agnes' invitation I continued living with her at her small farm.

Tiva and Ari were also valuable instructors who continued teaching me whenever they could. I found that after I was initiated I got to see Russell a lot more, which was always a pleasure. I always thought of him as a brother and when I crossed the initiation line he became a brother all over again in the tribal sense. I saw Russell's grandfather a fair bit too over the years and from him I learned things that lay both inside and outside of Thornish lore.

I finally had the chance to learn from Martin as well, though he was not the most socially active person and I saw him very little compared to the others. It was Martin who gifted me with a beautiful Shar and I will never forget that. He had a friend who was quite an accomplished blacksmith and metal worker and the beauty of the tool he gifted me with reflected that in an amazing way.

About three years after I completed my Seeker's Crossing I set out upon the Master's Deepening. This was a real eye-opener and was considerably different both in structure and experience than my first Deepening. In due time I was given another ritual and in this one I became a Master in the tradition. It was a huge honor and something I never would have imagined myself being able to do, but I did it…and survived to tell something of the tale.

For a number of years after my first initiation I continued to write things down and take notes about this thing or that within the tradition. I had no idea what I would do with my writing but I thought that at the very least I might have a kind of diary to look back on as the years passed by. Much of what was in those notes was locked in there because of the oaths I had taken and the secrecy which needed to be kept and in the end, after pondering it for a long time, I finally put down the pen. I decided I had said enough, told enough of the tale, and left off where I was in the hope that one day someone else or hopefully, several 'someone elses' might come along and take up the slack.

I think there is a lot left to be said about the Thornish way, even if that is solely concerned with the outer ring of the Thornwood. There is so much left to be told in this area and my story is but one tiny sliver of a much larger cultural pie.

The Thornish way is a thing which is very deep and primal on many levels and yet as an organic cultural being it is always growing, adapting and flowing with the times and the events going on around it. I have little doubt in my mind that when the new century comes, and it is not that far away now, only about fifteen years, my Thornish people will still be here, fighting the fight for balance and ever seeking the deeper wisdom as they always have.

This year I have had many adventures, not the least of which is the knowledge that I will one day soon be walking with the Dark Mother down the tunnel to the land of my ancestors. But in thinking about it I am neither afraid or regretful. I have learned much and gained much and as it goes in nature, the circle turns and I have also lost much. When we lost Ciarán I wondered how I could possibly go on. The farm house, now mine, was an empty, hollow shell, or so it seemed for a time.

A big part of my heart went to the spirit world with Ciarán and at the time I couldn't even imagine how I could survive that. But I did. I still had my tribal family and they were there for me when I had lost all hope.

Not only that, but new faces appeared and new folks began to walk in the way I had walked years before. This gave me focus and helped me to set aside the grief which for a time haunted me, even though as a Shar Master I should not have let the grief ride me so hard.

In 1990 I was again reminded of the sacred cycle when my dear friend Ari passed from this Middle World. He asked me to carry on without him and to teach what I was able to. It was his words, in large part, that caused me to dig out all of these old notes and once again set my mind to assembling them into some kind of useable order.

Life goes on and so should our traditions. Our numbers were never large though we hope to change that with more open teachings about our ways. As Ari said, the world needs defenders and in the Thornish people the sacred Dark Mother has created worthy implements for that purpose. I know that we are but one pagan tribal culture among the many that Ari predicted would re-emerge from the shadows and it is good to know we are not alone in our desire to serve that which is so very sacred.

Yet the Thornish way is unique in many aspects. It is, to paraphrase Agnes, the development of an ancient northern worldview which was planted respectfully in North American soil and allowed to grow. It has, as a result, many special aspects which may endear it to a specific kind of seeker.

As more people experience that spiritual and intellectual awakening (just as Ari predicted years ago) the need to find a road back to the ways of balance is desired by more people every day.

I hope that what I have written here will one day find its way out into the world and perhaps help those who are seeking, in one way or another.

Honor and respect,
Corva Ellensdottir
October, 1995

Afterword

The tradition that Corva describes so powerfully in this book has been in existence since November of 1958. On October 31st of that year, which Thornish people refer to as *Harrownight*, six men stood beside a fire in northern British Columbia, Canada. Here they laid the framework for what would become known as the Thornish pagan tradition and celebrated the creation of the first Thornish lodge, called the Raven Lodge.

This was not the first incarnation of what we now call the Thornish tradition. In the early years a wise and gifted man predicted that there would be three 'fires' or manifestations of this tribal experience. We are just now beginning to see the fulfillment of this prophecy.

The *First Fire* was the highly secretive Black Talon Society, a mutual protection order formed to keep what few pagan and Native traditions remained to them safe from the clutches of the overwhelming christianisation of those times. The *Second Fire*, so the prophecy has now proven, emerged with the formation of the Raven Lodge. This is the time that Corva speaks of. Still somewhat secretive and exclusive in many ways, the Thornish tradition grew and while it evolved and became different from the Old Lodges, it still held proudly to the core principles and ideas which were at the heart of its creation.

The manifestation known as the Second Fire continued for many years. But those within the tradition knew that this golden age would not last. They had seen that the Thornish tradition would face many challenges, carried forward into the new century by only a few remaining Thornsmen and Thornswomen.

The Farers also foresaw times ahead that would find many people returning to their pagan roots, the world-changing times in which we now live. They saw a world that would need those willing to work to return Balance to the world.

In nature, survival requires change and for the Thornish ways this change has been gradual. Though our numbers were never large it was decided to adopt a more open approach to sharing our ways. Thus the Thornish tradition has entered into what is now known as the time of the *Third Fire,* an adapted, somewhat more modern form of the tribal culture we have held for many years.

One of the few adaptations we have made is eliminating the divide between the Farers and the Spearfolk. There were many in the tradition who argued, even back in Raven's day, that requiring Seekers to make a choice between the two paths was unnecessarily divisive. There were some who chose one path and continued to learn from both. While we still have both Farers and Warriors, the Thornish tradition now advocates a more broad range of knowledge and practice.

This rekindled form of Thornish culture definitely contains the magic and the power of its predecessors, possibly more so, as it is the continuation of decades of work and dedication. We hope to kindle our fires even brighter than before and offer our teachings to those who find them of interest.

We have believed for many years now that a ReAwakening of the human spirit is upon the world. As Thornish tribal folk we know that more and more Earth-oriented tribal folk will rise to take up the defense of freedom, magic and life on our sacred home world. While we are only a single manifestation of such a spirit, we will carry our tradition forward in the changing times ahead.

Swords and spears are forged with heat and hammering. *Shar*—as Thornish initiates are called—are forged by trials and ordeals and tribal bonds. Challenging times, rough times—these tap into the deep vein of Bloodfire and bring forth those who are strong, who see through the Lies, who welcome the chance to restore Balance.

For more information on the Thornish tradition:

http://www.thornwoodpress.com/

Index

CPSIA information can be obtained
at www.ICGtesting.com
Printed in the USA
BVHW042342030919
557523BV00010B/263/P

9 781906 958916